The Ethic of Advocacy

Charles M. Masner

DISSERTATION.COM

Boca Raton

The Ethic of Advocacy

Dissertation.com
Boca Raton, Florida
USA • 2008

ISBN-10: 1-58112- 399-X
ISBN-13: 978-1-58112-399-9

THE ETHIC OF ADVOCACY

————————

A Dissertation

Presented to

The College of Education

University of Denver

————————

In Partial Fulfillment

of the Requirements for the Degree

Doctor of Philosophy

————————

by

Charles M. Masner

June 2007

Co-Chairs:
Dr. Kathy Green
Dr. Cynthia Hazel

TABLE OF CONTENTS

LIST OF TABLES

DEDICATION

This dissertation is dedicated to my parents, Charles William Masner and Ella Clotene Masner, without whose support this accomplishment would not have been possible

ACKNOWLEDGMENTS

I acknowledge the support of my dissertation Co-Chairs, Dr. Kathy Green and Dr. Cynthia Hazel. Dr. Hazel also served as my advisor. Dr. Green and Dr. Hazel spent considerable time and effort helping me complete this dissertation. I also acknowledge the support of the other members of my Dissertation Committee: Dr. Gloria Miller, Chair of the Child, Family and School Psychology Program in the University of Denver's College of Education; and Dr. Martin Tombari, Adjunct Faculty member in the College of Education, and my former advisor. In addition, I acknowledge the help of Dr. Roberto Corrada, of the University of Denver's College of Law, who served as chairperson for my Dissertation Defense. I thank all of these faculty members for their help.

I thank the focus group participants, the expert review panel participants, the cognitive interview participants, the pilot study participants, and the members of the Colorado Society of School Psychologists who participated in the study in chief, for the time and effort they gave to participate in this research. I also thank Dr. Nanci Avitable for her help in the compilation of the quantitative data in this study and Ms. Pat Corwin for her help in the final completion of the dissertation document.

CHAPTER I. INTRODUCTION

School psychologists have an ethical obligation to be advocates for children, according to the predominant professional organization for school psychologists, the National Association of School Psychologists (NASP, 2000). Although the NASP *Principles for Professional Ethics* state that school psychologists are to be advocates for children, the principles do not define advocacy, except through the inferences that may be drawn from what school psychologists must be, and do, in order to meet their ethical injunction to advocate for students. What is to be advocated for are the rights, welfare, needs, and best interests of the child who is a student, and who is the primary client of the school psychologist (NASP). For students who have certain disabilities, their rights, welfare, needs, and best interests are primarily defined by the Individuals With Disabilities Education Act (IDEA, 2004). These are students who meet 1 of the 13 disability categories of the IDEA and whose disability has an adverse impact on their learning so that they need specialized instruction. These students are legally entitled to a free appropriate public education (FAPE). Because students with disabilities are legally entitled to a FAPE, and because these students therefore have legal rights to be enforced, they are the students most in need of advocates to enforce those legal rights.

The focus of this study is on students covered by the IDEA. Although advocacy is also needed for children who are not of school age, that advocacy must take place, obviously, in non-school environments. Although advocacy for children in non-school environments is, also obviously, important, the school environment is the focus of this study because the school is the problematic public bureaucracy through which all children must eventually pass as students, unless, of course, they attend private schools. It is within this public-school bureaucracy that advocacy becomes most critical. In addition, although students with disabilities covered by Section 504 of the Rehabilitation Act of 1973 (Rehabilitation Act of 1973) are also entitled to a FAPE, the FAPE to which they are entitled only requires that their needs are met as adequately as their non-disabled peers (Chapman, 2000). Students with disabilities covered by the IDEA are legally entitled to more. However, effective advocacy for students covered by the IDEA can serve as a learning model for effective advocacy for students covered by Section 504, and, indeed, for all students.

Statement of the Problem

The ethical obligation of school psychologists to advocate for a FAPE for students with disabilities is a problem, because school psychologists are employees of bureaucracies, school districts, which are in turn composed of other employees, all of whom are accountable to school boards, which are in turn accountable to parents and voters. Thus, there will be competing views, and competing political powers in support of those views, in the process of

2

determining what should constitute the FAPE for which school psychologists, in their role as advocates, are ethically bound to seek for students with disabilities. The scope of the problem is substantial, because there are over 6 million students entitled to a FAPE under the IDEA (Bush, 2004).

The education of students with disabilities is affected as a result of how competing views are resolved about the meaning of the FAPE to which they are entitled. The education these students receive largely determines the quality of lives they will lead and the kind of democratic citizens they will be. Thus, the students' parents and other family members are also affected by the quality of the education that students with disabilities receive. The professional lives of the employees of the school district are affected. The lives of the students' non-disabled peers are affected. The budgets of school districts are affected. The lives of all citizens in a democratic society are affected by the quality of the education received by students with disabilities. The quality of this education is determined by the quality of the advocacy which promotes it.

If school psychologists do not satisfactorily meet their ethical obligation to be advocates for students with disabilities, the lives of students with disabilities may be diminished, because school psychologists have a depth and breadth of diagnostic and prognostic capabilities, as well as remediation capabilities, unequalled by any other school-system professional. School psychologists can be the key advocates within school systems for students with disabilities. However, if school psychologists do not live up to their ethical obligation to be advocates

3

for students with disabilities, there are no other actors within school systems who are as sufficiently qualified to fulfill this role, and to provide leadership in fulfilling this role.

Moreover, there is a more fundamental problem that this study addresses. The NASP *Principles for Professional Ethics* (hereafter referred to, interchangeably, as the NASP *Principles*) direct the school psychologists who are members of NASP to be advocates for students, but these principles do not define what advocacy means. Absent such definition, school psychologists who want to do their ethical best are left on their own to struggle with determining how to fulfill their role as advocates for students. The findings from this study will offer guidance about how advocacy is defined and perceived by practicing school psychologists, experts in school psychology, and advocacy experts.

The results of the survey portion of the study provide information about how prepared school psychologists believe they are to be advocates for students with disabilities. In addition, the survey results provide information about (a) the circumstances within which the ethical obligation for advocacy for individual students with disabilities manifests itself within the practice of school psychology; (b) the capabilities necessary for school psychologists to be effective advocates for individual students with disabilities; and (c) the barriers to, and the enablers of, effective advocacy by school psychologists on behalf of students with disabilities. Not to be clear about what the profession expects from school psychologists as advocates, when their ethical principles dictate that they be advocates, countenances not only ethical disaster for school psychologists, but

also educational disaster for the students whom they are ethically bound to serve.

Advocating for a Free Appropriate
Public Education (FAPE)

A FAPE is defined at 20 USC 1401(9) of the IDEA (2004) as:

> Special education and related services that - (A) have been provided at public expense, under public supervision and direction, and without charge; (B) meet the standards of the State educational agency; (C) include an appropriate preschool, elementary school, or secondary school education in the State involved, and; (D) are provided in conformity with the individualized education program required under [20 USC 1414(d)].

In addition, the United States Supreme Court, in *Board of Education v. Rowley, 458 U.S. 176* (1982), described the determination of the meaning of *appropriate* to be:

> First, has the State complied with the procedures set forth in the [IDEA]? And second, is the individualized educational program developed through the [IDEA's] procedures reasonably calculated to enable the child to receive educational benefits?

However, the Court's definition leaves undetermined the extent to which a

procedural violation will constitute a denial of a FAPE. Is failure to give notice of

an individualized educational program (IEP) meeting a denial of a FAPE?

Probably not, unless the parents fail to attend because of lack of notice, and the

result is an educational program to which the parents do not agree. However, even

when, as is usually the case, parents attend IEP meetings, there can be debate

about what an IEP "reasonably calculated to enable the child to receive

educational benefits" (*Board of Education v. Rowley,* 1982) means. Advocacy is critical to the determination of this meaning, as it is to the determination of all meaning, because advocacy is about persuading others to adopt a certain point of view, or to take certain actions: "Disagreements are not settled by the facts, but are the means by which the facts are settled" (Fish, 1980, p. 338).

A free appropriate public education (FAPE) is to be provided in the least restrictive environment (LRE). No student is to be rejected for eligibility and services due to the severity of the student's disability. The content of a FAPE in the LRE, as indicated by the federal statutory citation, and by the U.S. Supreme Court in *Board of Education v. Rowley*, is to be determined by an individualized education program (IEP). This IEP is to be based upon a non-discriminatory evaluation, with parent participation, and with procedural safeguards provided to the parents to insure the provision of a FAPE in the LRE to the student who is their son or daughter and who is covered by the Individuals With Disabilities Education Act (IDEA). These are the primary principles of the IDEA. As a public employee of the school district, the school psychologist is ethically and legally bound to advocate for a FAPE in the LRE, by upholding these principles, for all students covered by the IDEA.

However, because the IDEA is designed to avoid a one-size-fits-all approach to educating students with disabilities, and because educating students with disabilities can strain the resources of public school district budgets and staffs, school psychologists will inevitably encounter conflict in their role as advocates. Parents and school districts can, and often do, differ in their views about what constitutes a FAPE in the LRE for a student. Is 40 hours a week of an applied behavior approach appropriate for a student with autism? If the parents and the school district disagree on the answer to this question, what is the school psychologist's ethical obligation? In addition, what is the school psychologist's obligation when the needs of the student with autism conflict with the needs of another student? What does advocacy mean in this context, and therefore what does it mean for a school psychologist to be an advocate for students with disabilities covered by the IDEA?

The Advocacy Role of School Psychologists

Are school psychologists upholding the ethic of advocacy to seek a FAPE in the LRE for students? More fundamentally, do students need advocates? A lot of people inside and outside of public schools think so. In a book with a title that offers an explanation of why advocates for students with special needs are necessary, *Negotiating the Special Education Maze* (Anderson, Chitwood, & Hayden, 1997), the authors' quote one parent's frustration:

> I felt a very small and incidental part of [the IEP] procedure, and at times I felt that my daughter really wasn't getting her full share or placement of services. It wasn't until I started networking with other parents that I started feeling empowered to all the services you rightfully should have (p. ix).

As this parent indicates, parents can, and should be advocates for their children. But parents can get so emotional and so overwhelmed, in attempting to address their children's needs, that their ability to be effective advocates suffers, as experts in the field have recognized (Wright & Wright, 2002). Also, parents

7

often lack sufficient knowledge about special education law. Therefore, although parents should always be advocates for their children (Wright & Wright), parents sometimes need advocacy help, from inside, and from outside, the special education maze.

Lay advocates and attorney advocates can provide this help from outside school systems. Lay advocates and attorneys can go with parents to IEP meetings, and can otherwise help parents in their communications and relationships with school-system staff on behalf of students with disabilities. However, school-system staff are often defensive about the participation of lay advocates and attorneys, especially attorneys. Nonetheless, to the extent that advocacy requires formal dispute resolution such as litigation, attorney advocacy will be appropriate.

School personnel can provide advocacy help within school systems. Special education personnel in particular, including school psychologists, are the educational staff that historically have worked most closely with children with special needs, and continue to be most likely to have the knowledge necessary to advocate within school systems for the special needs of children. The Council for Exceptional Children (CEC, 2003), the predominant organization for special education professionals, includes advocacy for exceptional students (students with disabilities or students who are gifted) as one of its standards for professional practice. In addition, the National Association of Social Workers (NASW, 2002), in its standards for school social work services, includes as one of those standards advocacy for students and families.

The NASP *Principles for Professional Ethics* (2000) require school psychologists, in support of their ethical obligation to be advocates for children, to be knowledgeable about the "organization, philosophy, goals, objectives, and methodologies" (p. 26) of the school system. They are required to have an understanding of the "goals, processes, and legal requirements" (p. 26) of the school system. They should become "integral members" of the school-system. They are to make their views known to other school-system personnel. They are to promote change within school systems. Thus, the extent to which school psychologists will be effective advocates for students within school systems will depend on their ability to persuade others, which will in turn depend on (a) their diagnostic and remedial skills and knowledge; (b) their ability to present rational and caring arguments, which includes their social and political skills; and (c) their ethical character. In order for school psychologists to be effective problem solvers, consultants, and hence change agents doing their best to promote the best interests of students, school psychologists need to be effective practitioners of the art and science of persuasion.

Purpose of the Study

Being an advocate is a positive value. The authority for this conclusion is that being a child advocate is an ethical injunction included in the NASP *Principles for Professional Ethics* (2000). However, the NASP *Principles* do not adequately define what being a child advocate means for the practicing school psychologist. What is missing in the literature is a definition of advocacy for school psychologists and an appraisal of the perceptions of practicing school psychologists about the ethical admonition to be child advocates. This study offered a definition of child advocacy for school psychologists to evaluate, and explored the perceptions of school psychologists about their ethical responsibility to be advocates for the students with disabilities whom they serve. This study also explored the meaning school psychologists ascribe to the function of advocacy for improving the educational lives of students with disabilities in the public schools as viewed by practicing school psychologists. The perceptions of school psychologists have not been sufficiently assessed regarding their role in promoting this value. Such an assessment can help provide for better educating school psychologists about how to advocate more effectively and ethically on behalf of students.

Significance of the Study

The results of this study can be used to provide information and recommendations to NASP about how to better define the ethical admonition for school psychologists to be advocates. The study adds to the body of literature about the advocacy role of school psychologists by soliciting the expertise of practicing school psychologists about their role as advocates. Thus, the results can help provide better guidance to school psychologists about how to be effective advocates for students.

Research Questions

This study addresses these questions:

1. Do experts in school psychology, and practicing school psychologists, agree or disagree with the definition of advocacy presented by the researcher, and what changes, if any, would they make to that definition?

2. How prepared do experts in school psychology, and practicing school psychologists, believe school psychologists are to fulfill their ethical obligation to be advocates for individual students with disabilities?

3. As perceived by practicing school psychologists, and by school psychology experts, (a) what are the circumstances within which the ethical obligation for advocacy for individual students with disabilities manifests itself within the practice of school psychology, (b) what are the capabilities necessary for school psychologists to be effective advocates for individual students with disabilities, and (c) what are barriers to, and enablers of, effective advocacy by school psychologists on behalf of individual students with disabilities?

Definitions of Key Terms

Advocacy is the process of attempting to persuade others through logic, emotion, and ethical character. For a student with a disability covered by the Individuals With Disabilities Education Act (IDEA), advocacy is manifested in the creating and maintaining of a free appropriate public education (FAPE), in the

11

least restrictive environment (LRE), as determined through the process of creating and maintaining for that student an individualized education program (IEP). The focus of the researcher in this research is on advocacy for individual students, not systems advocacy.

The *Education for All Handicapped Children's Act (EAHCA)* is the federal law passed in 1975 providing for the education of students with disabilities. In 1990 it was renamed the Individuals With Disabilities Education Act (IDEA).

A *free appropriate public education (FAPE)* is that which is to be provided to students eligible to receive services under the IDEA. It is defined for each eligible student by the student's individualized education program (IEP).

The *Individuals With Disabilities Education Act (IDEA)* is the federal law that guarantees eligible students a FAPE. The most recent enactment is IDEA 2004, also known as the *Individuals With Disabilities Education Improvement Act (IDEIA)*.

An *individualized education program (IEP)* is the process and document through which a student eligible to receive a FAPE under the IDEA has that FAPE provided and defined.

The *least restrictive environment (LRE)* is the environment within which a student eligible under the IDEA to receive a FAPE is to receive that FAPE. It is a component of a FAPE. The LRE is generally understood to be the environment within which the student with a disability can best be included in the general education curriculum with his or her non-disabled peers. The decision about what constitutes the LRE, like the decision about what constitutes a FAPE, is determined by each student's IEP, which is created by a team composed of the student's parents, appropriate school district representatives, and, when appropriate, the student.

Persuasion, as used by the researcher, means influencing the attitudes or behaviors of others.

CHAPTER II. REVIEW OF THE LITERATURE

This literature review begins with a foundational description of advocacy. A historical overview of child advocacy is then provided. This is followed by a historical review of the role of the school psychologist as advocate: from the early years, through role reconsideration, to a proposed need for further research. A definition for advocacy for school psychologists is then proposed.

The Foundational History of Advocacy

The foundational recorded history of advocacy begins with Aristotle. To be a successful advocate is to be persuasive, and Aristotle judged the persuasive value of the rhetoric of speakers as being composed of three determinants. The better the speaker is able to convince the listener of the speaker's good character, the more persuasive the speaker will be. The better the speaker is able to appeal to the emotions of the listener, the more persuasive the speaker will be. The better the speaker is able to demonstrate the truth of what the speaker believes through the logic of rational argument, the more persuasive the speaker will be (trans.1984).

The foundational profession for advocacy is the law. The *Model Rules of Professional Conduct*, published by the American Bar Association (ABA, 2002), the predominant national professional organization for lawyers, devotes an entire rule to the lawyer's role as advocate. *Advocate* is defined by *Black's Law Dictionary* (2004) as "a person who assists, defends, pleads, or prosecutes for another" (p. 60). This same source defines advocacy as: "1. The work or profession of an advocate. 2. The act of pleading for or actively supporting a cause or proposal" (p.60).

Philosophy, as espoused in the words of Aristotle, and the profession of the law, are the two foundational pillars upon which the idea, and the practice, of advocacy have been given further construction by others who seek to practice advocacy, and to be advocates. In the modern history of education, including special education, these builders, these architects of advocacy, have proposed a variety of definitional designs for advocacy. However, the foundational pillars remain solid. Thus, Paul, Neufeld, and Pelosi (1977), educators and non-lawyers all, nonetheless sounded Aristotelian and lawyer-like when they wrote that "advocacy is representing or speaking for another person" (p. xi).

Child Advocacy

Paul (1977) argued for developing procedures for removing children from environments that worked against their best interests. He gave as examples circumstances that, although less prevalent today, nonetheless still merit our vigilant attention. One example was the circumstance of predominantly black children in predominantly white schools being placed in special education classes with the diagnostic label, "emotional disturbance." Another example was of a Hispanic child being placed in a class for the cognitively delayed, based upon an

English language intelligence test, when the child's primary language was Spanish.

Paul (1977) also argued for developing meaningful after-school activities for children. He argued for informing parents of their rights and alternatives when their child was to be given special services. He argued for providing special tutorial help to children that needed it. He argued for alternative living arrangements for children who were in abusive environments. He argued for the provision of appropriate community services to children when they needed them. He argued for providing an ombudsman to children who were involved in court proceedings. He argued for getting children out of jails. He argued for the deinstitutionalization of children. All of these arguments, according to Paul comprised the notion of what, in 1977, he believed was meant by *child advocacy*.

Westman (1979) wrote that the problems of children, and the remedies for those problems, often went undetected because the "child lack[ed] an advocate who [could] identify [the] child's needs and ensure that they [were] met" (p. xi). Westman described the essential characteristics of child advocacy as (a) helping children build bridges with the cultural systems of which they were a part, (b) helping children to develop appropriately, (c) helping to better resolve conflicts about what is best for children, (d) fostering more appropriate development of the facts regarding the needs of children, and (e) being better able to work with multiple disciplines on behalf of children. According to Westman, an ethical child advocate needed to assume a degree of responsibility for the child, ensure that interventions did no harm, and not inappropriately foster dependence in the child.

Describing advocacy for children within educational systems, Westman wrote,

> The essence of child advocacy in education is infusing the educational system with elements of the health and legal systems. Because advocacy for a child focuses the resources of the educational system on an individual, it may encounter basic resistance in the system. Paradoxically, a child advocate may be a foreign body in the educational system, because the system is generally equipped to process groups of children rather than treat or represent individuals (p. 205).

Thus, according to Westman (1979), child advocacy required focusing on students as individuals within educational systems. But, such advocacy could also expect resistance, because the dynamics of educational systems were better at attending to groups of children, rather than individual children.

Herr (1991) described child advocacy in special education as an attempt "to make school bureaucracies more responsive to the law's idealistic norms and the child's individual needs" (p. 151). He described the agenda for such advocacy to be

- Ensuring the inclusion of all students with disabilities in educational systems;

- Increasing the fairness in identifying, evaluating, and placing students with disabilities;

- Improving the quality of special education services through individual programming, increased resources, better training of staff, and improved technologies;

- Increasing parent and student participation in decision making;

- Giving more visibility and legitimacy to including children in the general education curriculum;

- Questioning assumptions and operating practices to determine whether they were based on administrative convenience rather than designed to serve the needs of students.

Fiedler (2000), in prefacing his argument for special education advocacy, by special education professionals, on behalf of children with special needs, listed definitions of advocacy and advocate that had been provided by other authors:

> Advocacy … means seeing that one's own organization plans with people rather than just for them, and is sufficiently representative of groups to be served that planning with them is possible. It means changing by-laws, scrapping policies, changing procedures that are part of the problem rather than a part of the solution. It means orienting the service delivery to the consumers in terms of time, place, type of services, type of staff and attitude. It means using the power we have. It may mean altering or holding in abeyance the agenda of the client group (Riley, as cited in Fiedler, p. 2).

> Advocacy is intervention when needed services are not accessible; are not available; are not appropriate; are not effectively provided; or when the voice of a child is not being heard (Herbert & Mould, as cited in Fiedler, p. 3).

> Advocacy is a problem-solving strategy to correct problems in service delivery (Hines, as cited in Fielder, p. 3).

> An advocate is someone who acts on behalf of or for another person's cause (Alper, Schloss, & Schloss, as cited in Fiedler, p. 3).

> An advocate [is] a person who speaks on behalf of or in partnership with someone else, such as a child or parent, in order to procure needed services (Stoecklin, as cited in Fiedler, p. 3).

> Advocacy is defined as information, advice and representation provided to individuals and their families to assist them to acquire appropriate services for a person with a disability (Bonney & Moore, as cited in Fiedler, p. 3).

Child advocacy is intervention on behalf of children in relation to those services and systems that are injurious to children, that are inadequate to prevent harm, or that provide inappropriate help to children (Cahill, as cited in Fiedler, p. 3).

An advocate is one who speaks on behalf of another person or group of persons in order to bring about change (Anderson et al., as cited in Fiedler, p. 3).

Out of these definitions, Fiedler (2000) identified the following characteristics of advocacy for children with disabilities: (a) the first allegiance of an advocate is to the person for whom he or she is advocating, not the advocate's employer; (b) advocacy usually means seeking to change the status quo; (c) advocates speak up for individuals, perhaps in concert with fellow advocates; and (d) the intent of advocacy is to correct identified problems or to otherwise improve services for children with disabilities. Of the first characteristic, Fiedler wrote,

An advocate's primary allegiance or loyalty must be to children with disabilities and their families. In this allegiance, special education professionals face potential conflicts of interest in their advocacy in that they are employees of a school district that they may be challenging. Their primary commitment, however, ethically rests with children and families (p. 3).

Advocates employed by school districts owe a duty to their employer. However, their primary duty is to the students, and their families, whom they are serving as advocates.

With regard to what he identified as the second characteristic of advocacy, changing the status quo, Fiedler (2000) argued that such advocacy required "professional dedication, time, energy, and a clear vision of desired outcomes"

19

(p. 3). Speaking up for individuals, Fiedler's third characteristic of advocacy, required, he argued, that advocates work to "empower parents" (p. 3) to be advocates for their children. The fourth characteristic of advocacy, identifying problems and improving services, according to Fiedler, required advocates to determine the manner in which to address the problems identified in order to improve "educational systems and services for children with disabilities and their families" (p. 3).

Wright and Wright (2002) argued that special education advocacy was not a mysterious process. They argued that advocates gather information about the student's disability and educational history in order to help resolve disagreements with school systems. Advocates educate themselves about how decisions are made within school systems, and by whom, and advocates are knowledgeable about the legal rights of students with disabilities. Advocates plan and prepare for interactions with school staff. Advocates keep written records that document what has happened with regard to decision making for a student with a disability. Advocates are not afraid to ask questions of school-district staff, and they are good listeners. Advocates are proactive in identifying student problems. Advocates propose solutions for student problems. Regarding school staff as advocates, Wright and Wright wrote,

> Teachers and special education providers often view themselves as advocates. Teachers, administrators, and school staff may provide support to children and their families. Because they are employed by school districts, it is unlikely that school personnel can advocate for children with disabilities without endangering their jobs. (p. 5)

20

Wright and Wright (2002) give qualified support to the view that school staff can be advocates for children and their families. The qualification is that this advocacy may be circumscribed by the realization by school staff that advocacy for students may be job threatening.

The Council for Exceptional Children (CEC, 2003) describes the role of the special education professional advocate as "speaking, writing, and acting" (p. 3) on behalf of exceptional students. The National Association for Social Workers (NASW, 2002) describes the role of the school social worker student advocate as "support[ing] [student] needs" (p. 13). The American Psychological Association (APA, 2002), which has a Division 16 for school psychologists, does not mention the word advocate or advocacy in its *Ethical Principles of Psychologists and Code of Conduct*, although the provisions of that document are arguably not inconsistent with the role of advocate or the process of advocacy. The predominant professional organization for school psychologists, the National Association of School Psychologists (NASP, 2002), expressly describes the role of the school psychologist advocate for students as requiring that "school psychologists 'speak up' for the needs and rights of their students/clients even at times when it may be difficult to do so" (p. 13).

However, the ability and obligation of special education professionals, school social workers, and school psychologists to function as advocates for students with disabilities within school systems has required the participation of advocates external to the school system. That participation was required in order

21

to obtain legal authority to support the manifestation of the advocacy abilities and obligations of internal school-system advocates.

In 1972, the landmark federal district court cases of *Mills v. District of Columbia Board of Education* (1972) and *Pennsylvania Association for Retarded Citizens* (PARC) *v. Commonwealth of Pennsylvania* (1972) were decided, providing federal court precedents for the rights of children with disabilities. The year 1972 was just 3 years prior to the passage of the Education for All Handicapped Children's Act (EAHCA), renamed in 1990 as the Individuals With Disabilities Education Act (IDEA). The NASP *Principles for Professional Ethics* were adopted in 1974, and more explicit child advocacy provisions were incorporated in 1992.

The Early Years of the School Psychologist
as Advocate: Role Definition

The modern day invocation of the term *child advocacy* became more common beginning in 1969 with a published report of the Joint Commission on the Mental Health of Children (Knitzer, 1976). Then, in 1972, the year *Mills* and *Pennsylvania Association for Retarded Citizens* (*PARC*), were decided, Catterall and Hinds (1972) advocated for the role of school psychologist to be that of a child advocate. They based their argument on a determination that the historical justification for school psychologists had altered, making necessary a new justification. Historically, according to the authors, school psychologists had been used as testers whose primary task it was to identify those with cognitive disabilities, what was then termed *mental retardation*. Over time, this role changed to meet the more diverse needs of students. Nonetheless, the

stereotypical role of the school psychologist as one who gave tests, especially IQ

tests, remained. Testing, however, was increasingly under attack as being biased

against minority cultural groups. Another trend was toward keeping students with

disabilities in the regular classroom, rather than providing them with educational

services more separate from their non-disabled peers. Also, adequate funding for

services for students with special needs was increasingly becoming more of a

problem. For these reasons, Catterall and Hinds believed that school psychologists

needed to be able to demonstrate a new problem-solving professional identity and

public image.

Catterall and Hinds (1972) discussed three potential roles for school

psychologists: change agents, ombudsmen, and child advocates. Although the

functions of these roles overlap, the authors concluded that child advocate was the

preferred role. According to Catterall and Hinds, "The concept of 'change for

change's sake' [was] probably losing popularity and would have definite

disadvantages as a long-range public relations campaign" (p. 17). The concept of

ombudsmen (a Swedish term that uses the male gender even though it was not

intended to be gender specific) was recognized by Catterall and Hinds as "one of

giving someone within the system the authority to stand up strongly for the rights

of the student" (p. 18). The authors concluded that, although the term had had its

advantages, it seemed "rather distant and intellectual and the concept would tend

to be hard to explain to the general public" (p. 18). Furthermore, "it [did] not clearly bring into focus those aspects of [school psychology] training in the behavioral sciences that would make school psychologists good Ombudsmen" (p. 18). The authors argued for the role definition of child advocate for school psychologists, because they thought it would be better received by the public than a role definition of change agent or ombudsman. Also, Catterall and Hinds thought that school psychologists had special expertise in the behavioral sciences that was not adequately reflected in the role definition of an ombudsman.

Catterall and Hinds (1972) determined that *child advocate* was the most appropriate role definition for a school psychologist. They stated that "the psychologist typically describes his primary goal as the optimal educational and emotional development of each child" (p. 18). Therefore, according to Catterall and Hinds, the school psychologist acts as a child advocate within the educational system as an attorney acts for his or her client within the justice system. A student does not always meet the academic and behavioral expectations of the school system. The reasons for these failures will always be, of course, in part, unique to the student who does not meet these expectations. Students have special needs that the school district seeks to meet. The ability of the school district to do so is increased, according to Catterall and Hinds, if the student has a school psychologist advocate to help in clarifying the student's needs, and to make sure that a full continuum of interventions to meet those needs is considered.

Catterall and Hinds (1972) argued for the school psychologist as child advocate as a "third force" between teachers and school administrators (1972, p.

24

21). The authors concluded, "In short, a Child Advocate could come out strongly for each child's total *right to learn* – both intellectually and emotionally" (p. 21). In so arguing, Catterall and Hinds concluded that a third force, arguing for a student's right to learn, both intellectually and emotionally, was necessary. Necessary because neither classroom teachers nor school administrators were in a position to "put all the pieces together" (p. 21). However, the school psychologist, as child advocate, could "develop and use communication skills which would mobilize all of the significant people in a child's life to 'put all the pieces together,' and to build a plan that would be best for all" (p. 21).

Without citing Catterall and Hinds, Mearig (1974) argued forcefully that training for child advocacy should be an integral part of professional development for school psychologists: "Training for child advocacy has to occur as an inherent part of professional development, perhaps even requiring values which go back to early development and education" (p. 125). According to Mearig, "Advocacy cannot be tacked onto a curriculum" (p. 125). Mearig argued that the education of school psychologists must emphasize, as a part of the philosophical foundation of that education, that school psychologists not only be well informed about the steps necessary to help children maximize their potential, but also have a commitment to seeing that such steps are actually taken. Therefore, according to Mearig, school psychologists should experience, as a part of their professional education, practice in child advocacy that includes risk taking and experience in coping with conflict.

Hyman and Schreiber (1974) were consistent in the belief that the school psychologist must advocate for the child, and that maintaining this advocacy would not be easy. "Almost all school psychologists consider themselves to be child advocates" (p. 21), wrote Hyman and Schreiber, but, too often, "their idealism diminishes as they try to cope with the everyday pressures and politics of practice" (p. 21). This occurred as school psychologists encountered school employees who resisted helping children with special needs. Nonetheless, according to the authors: "The school psychologist is and must be a child advocate" (p. 50).

Hyman and Schreiber (1977) argued that the child, not the school system, was the school psychologist's major client. They further argued that the APA and NASP codes of ethics supported this view. They rejected a role for the school psychologist of neutral ombudsman, arguing that school psychologists must be focused on advocacy for students. They recognized that this might sometimes require that school psychologists be adversarial with their school district employers: "Although we do not believe that confrontation is the preferred method for guaranteeing children's rights, we do not reject this method; confrontation must be judiciously used and focused correctly" (p. 8). Advocacy for a child in an educational system sometimes requires that resources be expended on that child disproportionately to other students in the system, and thus the system may resist that expenditure (Westman, 1979). Confrontation may be an unavoidable part of such advocacy. Advocacy for students requires a diagnostic concern with the resolution of conflict in school systems (Chesler, Bryant, & Crowfoot, 1976). Advocacy for students accepts that students have individual differences, and advocates working on behalf of individual students may sometimes need to work to help school staff members learn how to best respond to the individual differences of those students (Svec, 1990). A willingness to confront the powers of school systems, a willingness to engage in the resolution of conflict, and a willingness to address individual differences are critical to providing a FAPE for students with disabilities.

The School Psychologist as Advocate:
Role Reconsideration

McMahon (1993) wrote that the momentum of the general child advocacy movement of the early 1970s was the context in which the profession of school psychology adopted without reservation the concept of school psychologist as child advocate. However, notwithstanding the political-action efforts of professional organizations aligned with school psychologists, the subsequent political conservatism of the 1980s otherwise diminished interest in an advocacy model for school psychology practice. Writing in 1993, McMahon stated that "few school psychologists [had] received formal instruction in the theory and practice of child advocacy" (p. 745). McMahon offered this conceptual definition of child advocacy:

> To successfully integrate advocacy services, school psychologists must adopt a particular view of the world. From the beginning, we must recognize that children have rights to both self-determination and protection from harm that evolve from their unique position within society (Melton; Rogers & Wrightsman; United Nations; as cited in McMahon, p.

27

745). As idealists, we must believe that children are entitled, without question, to an educational experience that contributes optimally to their development as individuals (Hart & Pavlovic; Prasse; as cited in McMahon, p. 745). As realists, we must expect that inequitable distribution of resources, limited access to opportunity, neglect of professional responsibility, and the general nature of bureaucratic organizations will, at times, deny children the education to which they are entitled (Kahn et al., as cited in McMahon, p. 745). When we see this happening, being an advocate means recognizing that, because they have virtually no power within educational systems, children will need assistance securing quality services from unresponsive institutions. From this perspective, being an advocate means becoming involved in a never ending search for ways to change schools so that they provide all children with an education that contributes meaningfully to their physical, psychological, and social development (McMahon, p. 746).

McMahon's definition recognizes the importance, notwithstanding the difficulty, of school psychologists being advocates for children.

McMahon (1993) identified the desirable qualities of a successful advocate as being "the ability to cope with ambiguity, the strength to stand alone, tolerance for criticism, the ability to resist institutional pressure to compromise personal beliefs, and the ability to see the system through the eyes of the client" (p. 752). Thus, as earlier authors had indicated, child advocacy needed to be "oriented to assisting in negotiations between children, the adults who interact with children, and the system" (Paul, 1977, p. 9). Moreover, according to Westman (1991), child advocacy should be a "state of mind" (p. xxi) guiding actions on behalf of children. According to McMahon, the successful advocate also needed "a secure sense of self, ...a stable professional identity, and ... emotional support outside the work place" (p. 752).

The School Psychologist as Advocate:
A Role in Need of Research

In 1999, Jacob-Timm presented the results of a systematic attempt to

understand the ethical views of practicing school psychologists. The study used

the critical-incident-technique method that has the advantage of letting the

respondents identify the ethical dilemmas, but the disadvantage that it usually

yields a low return rate (Jacob-Timm). Jacob-Timm divided the ethical dilemma

responses into 19 categories, based upon area of concern. All of these categories

could be said to impinge upon the school psychologist's ethic of advocacy for his

or her primary client, the child. However, the category of ethical dilemmas in

which this most frequently occurred involved situations in which school

psychologists felt administrative pressure to put the interests of the school district

ahead of the interests of the individual student. And, within this category, the

greatest source of reported conflict between administrators and school

psychologists (20 incidents) was regarding decisions about special education

eligibility, placement, and services, especially out-of-district private placements.

One school psychologist, quoted by Jacob-Timm, reported,

> A general dilemma which occurs locally is one which is budgetarily
> motivated. With ever decreasing financial resources, school administrators
> have become more aware of the cost of placing children with special needs
> out-of-district. For the school psychologist, this poses a dilemma when the
> administrator puts pressure on the psychologist to recommend in-district
> placement. Does the school psychologist recommend what the test results
> indicate or what the district prefers? While it is clear that we work in the
> students' best interest, this does pose a dilemma (p. 209).

Jacob-Timm (1999) concluded, "Findings from the present study thus support the view that, in addition to knowledge of the content of ethical codes, ethical problem-solving skills need to be explicitly taught" (pp. 215-216). It was also her belief that the reports she gathered could be helpful in both ethics education and the development of a structured questionnaire for further research on the ethical problems of practicing school psychologists. The ethic of advocacy is a problem for school psychologists that can benefit from such research.

The School Psychologist as Advocate:
A Proposed Definition

School psychologists, as advocates, have an ethical obligation to "speak up" on behalf of students, including students with special needs who are entitled to a free appropriate public education (FAPE) (NASP, 2000, p. 13). Speaking up, to be effective as advocacy, must be persuasive. Advocacy is the process of attempting to persuade others through logic, emotion, and ethical character. Of these three, the most fundamental is ethical character, because appropriate ethical character requires that school psychologists be committed, as the NASP *Principles* require, to being advocates for students, and that school psychologists be perceived as being persons of appropriate ethical character who advocate on behalf of students. Once school psychologists accept the obligation to be ethical advocates for students, school psychologists must also commit themselves to otherwise becoming effective speakers on behalf of students, if they are to be effective advocates for these students. For students with disabilities covered by the IDEA, this includes developing and maintaining the capabilities necessary to participate in rational and caring conversations about how to create and maintain individualized education programs (IEPs) that provide these students with disabilities a free appropriate public education (FAPE) in the least restrictive environment (LRE).

CHAPTER III. METHOD

A mixed research design was selected as the best method available to research a proposed definition for advocacy for children with disabilities and to research the perceptions of school psychologists about their role as advocates. This chapter lists the research questions addressed by the survey, and describes the survey research design selected and the participants. This chapter also describes the chronology of steps undertaken in conducting the study, the focus group process for discussing a proposed definition of child advocacy for students with disabilities, the development of the survey instrument, the procedures for administration of the survey, and data analysis. The results of the processes for construction of the final survey questionnaire are provided. The survey questionnaire items for each research question, and reliability coefficients, are found in Appendix L.

The Research Questions

1. Do experts in school psychology, and practicing school psychologists, agree or disagree with the definition of advocacy presented by the researcher, and what changes, if any, would they make to that definition?

2. How prepared do experts in school psychology, and practicing school psychologists, believe school psychologists are to fulfill their ethical obligation to be advocates for individual students with disabilities?

3. As perceived by practicing school psychologists, and by school psychology experts, (a) what are the circumstances within which the ethical obligation for advocacy for individual students with disabilities manifests itself within the practice of school psychology; (b) what are the capabilities necessary for school psychologists to be effective advocates for individual students with disabilities; and (c) what are barriers to, and enablers of, effective advocacy by school psychologists on behalf of individual students with disabilities?

Justification for the Design

One way to determine the perceptions of school psychologists about their ethical role as advocates for students with disabilities, other than interviewing each of them individually, was to do a census survey of the membership of the Colorado Society of School Psychologists (CSSP). Because no definition of advocacy exists in the NASP *Principles for Professional Ethics*, it was also determined by the researcher that it would be appropriate to research a proposed definition of advocacy through a focus group of school psychology experts.

Chronology of the Study

Chronologically, the study was conducted as follows:

Step 1: A focus group of 7 school psychologist experts was convened to respond to a proposed definition of child advocacy for school psychologists;

Step 2: A list of potential questionnaire items was created, based upon the focus group discussion and the literature review; and these questionnaire items were reviewed by a panel of 6 experts in advocacy, with potential questionnaire items being eliminated or added based upon this expert review;

Step 3: Cognitive interviews were conducted, using the potential questionnaire items identified or added after the expert review, with 3 practicing school psychologists in Colorado, with potential questionnaire items being modified based upon these cognitive interviews;

Step 4: A questionnaire, created through the filters of the focus group, expert panel, and cognitive interview processes, was pilot-tested with 21 convenience sampled practicing school psychologists in Colorado;

Step 5: The data from the pilot study were collected;

Step 6: The data from the pilot study were analyzed;

Step 7: The study-in-chief questionnaire was prepared;

Step 8: The study-in-chief questionnaire was administered to the membership of the Colorado Society of School Psychologists (CSSP);

Step 9: The data from the study-in-chief questionnaire were collected;

Step 10: The data from the study-in-chief were analyzed.

Step 1: The Focus Group

The focus group was composed of 7 experts in school psychology, convenience sampled by the researcher. The participation of these experts was by personal invitation of the researcher. They were contacted in person, by telephone, or by email. The criteria for selection of the focus group participants was that he or she (a) be a school psychologist licensed in Colorado; (b) have a minimum of 5 years of practice as a school psychologist; (c) be a member of the National Association of School Psychologists (NASP) and the Colorado Society of School Psychologists (CSSP); and (d) have the recommendation of the Colorado Department of Education's (CDE) School Psychology Consultant or the recommendation of a trainer of school psychologists at one of Colorado's graduate programs in school psychology. All focus group participants met these criteria.

The focus group was conducted in Vail, Colorado, on October 5, 2005, in conjunction with the CSSP annual convention. The focus group lasted approximately 2 hours.

The focus group began with the presentation, explanation, and signing of consent forms (see Appendix A), followed by introductions, according to a focus group protocol (see Appendix B). Participants introduced themselves to each other and described their current and past work experience in school psychology as a part of the introductions. About 15 minutes was allowed for introductions. The purpose of the focus group, to research the response of school psychology

35

experts to a proposed definition for advocacy by school psychologists for students with disabilities, was explained to the participants. This took about 15 minutes. Included in this explanation was a request to have the participants provide their honest perceptions. It was also explained to the participants that the focus group was part of a dissertation study. Their role was explained as helping, through discussion questions prepared by the researcher, to research a proposed definition of child advocacy for school psychologists, for use in a survey to be conducted with a random sample of the membership of the National Association of School Psychologists. The survey was later changed to a census survey of the membership of CSSP, when access to the NASP membership list was not obtained. With the consent of the participants, the focus group was audio-taped and transcribed. Quotes were verbatim, unless otherwise noted, except as edited for readability by the researcher.

Discussion questions for the focus group participants were developed by the researcher, based upon his literature review (see Appendix C). Approximately 90 minutes were allowed for discussion. The focus group questions were as follows:

- Do you think being a child advocate is an appropriate ethical principle for school psychologists? Why or why not?

- Please share your views of the qualities necessary for school psychologists to be effective child advocates.

- Please share your views about how the practice of child advocacy by school psychologists could be improved.

- Please respond to the proposed definition of child advocacy for school psychologists.

All of the focus group participants indicated that being a child advocate was an appropriate ethical principle for school psychologists. As one school psychologist said, "I believe that everything we're doing is for kids, well, especially for kids who have disabilities. That seems to be our primary reason that we're hired." And, as another school psychologist said,

> I think we're in a unique position to be advocates, for a lot of reasons. Our scope of training is broader than most other educators that we come in contact with and we're in a position where people look up to us to make a lot of difficult decisions, and I think that that's part of the reason why we're in such a good place to become the advocate, the primary advocate for children.

And another, "I think advocacy is basically our prime reason for being in the profession." On the other hand, all also agreed with what one of the focus group participants said, "There's times where school psychologists have to remain neutral, and I think they've been well trained to do that. And to be supportive and good listeners. And not take sides. Especially in terms of parents."

The focus group participants had a variety of responses to the question of the qualities they thought necessary for school psychologists to be effective child advocates. One stated, "One of them is courage. I think there are times when, especially in contentious situations around children, being willing to speak up about a child's needs is the first step." The participants also used words such as assertiveness, sensitivity, negotiator, collaborator, mediator, consultant, team member, confidence, flexibility, empathy, care, trust, and reasoned concern, to describe their views of the qualities necessary for a school psychologist to be an effective child advocate.

The focus group participants were next asked how they thought the practice of child advocacy could be improved. All agreed with one participant who said, "I think that the foundations of, the principles of, ethics, and advocacy, need to be taught at some level." Another said school psychologists had to re-commit to "getting a better understanding of a child we're advocating for." One participant mentioned "good mentoring." Another said, "I don't recall, my training was awhile ago, but I don't recall advocacy being taught." All agreed that supportive supervision and administration were helpful.

When asked to specifically respond to the researcher's proposed definition of advocacy, all of the focus group participants agreed that they were advocates for all students. How ethical character was to be defined was a focus of this discussion. The participants offered their views of their understanding of "ethical character," with one stating, "Ethical character means what other people are perceiving your own ethics to be," and another stating, "We have an ethical obligation to be effective advocates." Other participants were uncertain about how ethical character should otherwise be defined.

Step 2: The Expert Panel

A list of potential questionnaire items was created, by the researcher, based upon the focus group discussion and the researcher's literature review. The list of potential questionnaire items was reviewed by 6 Colorado experts in advocacy, including school psychologists, attorneys, and lay person advocates. The experts were identified by the researcher and contacted by personal invitation of the researcher, either in person or by telephone or email communication.

The experts who were school psychologists were selected using the same criteria as was used for the focus group participants. The criteria for selecting the attorney experts were that (a) he or she be licensed to practice law in the state of Colorado; (b) have at least 5 years experience representing either parents or school districts in special education issues; and (c) have a recommendation from an opposing attorney advocate or a recommendation from a hearing officer in Colorado in front of whom the recommended attorney advocate had appeared in a special education dispute. The criteria for selecting lay person advocates were that he or she have (a) at least 5 years of experience in Colorado as a lay advocate for students with disabilities and their families and (b) have a recommendation from either an appropriate representative of the Legal Center for People with Disabilities or the Arc of Colorado (both of which are non-profit advocacy organizations for persons with disabilities in Colorado), or a recommendation from an appropriate representative of another advocacy organization for persons with disabilities in Colorado that is recognized by either the Legal Center or the Arc. All experts signed IRB-approved consent forms (see Appendix D).

The experts were asked to eliminate, add, or clarify prospective questionnaire items (see Appendix J). The experts completed this task over a period of approximately 2 months.

There were 80 prospective closed-ended questionnaire items and 5 prospective open-ended questionnaire items. Most prospective questionnaire items received no comment. These items, or the substance of their subject matter, remained in the pool of potential questionnaire items. The experts did, however, raise substantive, as well as procedural, objections to some questionnaire items. However, their reviews did not indicate consensus, and varied according to their advocacy perspective. For those items where the expert's objection was clarity of the item, the item was either eliminated, or reworded, if, in the latter case, it was included in the draft of the questionnaire used for the cognitive interviews. So, for example, an item which read, "An advocate interprets the world for others," was eliminated. However, another prospective item, which read, "School psychologists should be educated about how to be successful child advocates," was not eliminated, even though the school psychologist expert who reviewed the item stated, "Advocacy is one aspect of our role, but my concern is the potential perception that we are only child advocates." This item was substantive to the researcher's project, notwithstanding the school psychologist's concern, and remained in the item pool, albeit with the word "child" dropped from the final version of the item.

The other school psychologist expert objected to an item in the item pool which read, "A school psychologist child advocate must be professionally competent," because the expert found the term, "competent," vague. This item was dropped from the prospective item pool. On the other hand, this same school psychologist objected to an item which read, "As a school psychologist, if conflicts exist between my student clients and any other clients I may have, my primary obligation is to my student clients." The school psychologist objected stating that in a school setting, "someone could argue that technically our only clients are students." The researcher left versions of this item in the item pool, because the dynamic of who the client is for the school psychologist is one of the dynamics of determining the meaning of being a school psychologist advocate, which was a part of the researcher's research project.

The parent lay advocate recognized the problem of this dynamic in commenting on the prospective item, "As a school psychologist, my primary clients are students." The parent offered an item which read, "As a school psychologist, the parents of my student clients can also be my clients." A version of this item offered by the parent was added to the item pool. The other lay advocate, and a person with a disability, also recognized this problem in commenting on the prospective item which read, "The primary client of a school psychologist is the child, not the school system." The lay advocate characterized this item as the "$25,000 question." Versions of this item remained in the item pool.

One of the attorney experts commented on the prospective item, "As a school psychologist, my primary clients are students," as follows:

> This assumes that students are "clients" at all. Isn't that a question that needs to be answered before we get to the issue of which two "clients" is "primary"? How would you define "client"? For example, there is no psychologist-patient privilege between a school psychologist and any student. How could the student be a "client" in that context? We talk about those served by any governmental agency or program as being "clients" of that agency or program. But the service is within the context of the specific mandate of the agency or program, and does not go beyond that mandate. To go beyond the agency mandate on behalf of a particular individual "client" is a way of stealing resources and services from other agency "clients" and from the public. I think you need some questions that air this issue.

The NASP *Principles for Professional Ethics* (2000) state that students and others can be clients of school psychologists, and that when conflicts exist between multiple clients of a school psychologist the primary client should be the student. The attorney's response, however, indicates, as did the responses of other experts, the problematic of determining who is the client, for the purpose of fulfilling the school psychologist's ethical obligation to be an advocate. The researcher therefore did indeed include items in the questionnaire that aired this issue.

This same attorney expert found problematic the use of the word "rights" in prospective items, commenting that it presumed that rights could be in conflict. The attorney preferred the prospective item which read, "In order to be effective child advocates, school psychologists must sometimes place the needs of students above the needs of the school system." The attorney stated, "I like this. When you talk 'needs' instead of 'rights,' the question becomes more interesting. Another way of putting it might be, 'rights' of the student above the 'needs' or 'interests' of the school district." The researcher agreed, and reconstructed prospective questionnaire items accordingly.

Step 3: The Cognitive Interviews

The researcher identified 3 practicing school psychologists in the state of Colorado to participate in cognitive interviews. The researcher personally invited the interviewees to participate in the study, either in person, or by telephone conversation or email. The researcher met with the interviewees individually and asked them to complete the survey and tell the researcher what they were thinking as they did so, followed by probing questions as necessary. The interviews were audio-taped.

Prior to the interviews, consent forms were explained, and written consents were obtained from all interviewees (see Appendix F). All interviews took place at a time convenient for the interviewees, at their respective work locations, in an available room of their choosing. Each interview lasted about one hour. The researcher then reviewed the audio-tapes of the interviews and the researcher's notes, and reduced the list of survey items to an appropriate number, and otherwise modified the questionnaire as necessary, based upon the feedback from the interviewees, for the purpose of preparing the items for the participants in the pilot study.

43

Modification of the Questionnaire

Based upon the information gained from the 3 school psychologists who participated in the cognitive interviews, the questionnaire was modified as follows:

Items 40 and 41. Item 40 originally read, "A school psychologist advocate should recommend needed services for a student, regardless of whether the employing school district has those services available." Item 41 originally read, "A school psychologist advocate should recommend a needed private placement for a student, regardless of cost." One of the school psychologists struggled with who was determining the "need" component in these items. The items were reworded to make clear that need, for the purpose of responding to these items, was based upon the belief of the school psychologist.

Item 42. Item 42 was changed to make the second "student" in this item plural.

Item 47. Item 47 was changed by deleting the clause, "not employed by school districts," and substituting the clause, "who are employed in different settings." This change was made because two of the school psychologists were confused about what "not employed by school districts" meant.

Item 51. Item 51 originally read, "A school psychologist advocate should be open to being persuaded by the logic, emotion, and ethical character of others advocating on behalf of students." The wording, "the logic, emotion, and ethical character," was deleted, because one of the school psychologists found it difficult to respond to each of these qualities together in one item.

Item 56. The second and final open-ended item, Item 56, originally read, "The Proposed Definition for the School Psychologist as Advocate, would be appropriate for all students, if all students were on IEPs." All of the school psychologist interviewees had some problem with the wording of this item. One of them wanted to delete the clause, "if all students were on IEPs." However, as another interviewee pointed out, doing so did not solve the problem, because there was a difference in the legal status of IDEA students and non-IDEA students in the public schools. Also, all 3 of the school psychologist interviewees pointed out that you could have non-IDEA students on IEPs, and still not have their legal status be the same. The item was therefore reworded to posit more clearly the same potential legal status for non-IDEA students as for IDEA students.

Item 57. One of the interviewees suggested changing two of the ethnic descriptors in Item 57 as follows: Latino/a for Hispanic, and Anglo for White. These changes were made.

All of the interviewees were asked what they thought about the length of the questionnaire, and none of them indicated that they found the length onerous. The interviewees also indicated that they found the questionnaire items understandable, with the exceptions of the specific items that the researcher has discussed.

Step 4: The Pilot Study

The participants in the pilot study were a convenience sample of 21 practicing school psychologists in the state of Colorado, selected by the researcher. They were asked to participate by personal invitation of the researcher, either in person, by telephone call, by email, or by regular mail. All questionnaires in the pilot study were either mailed to the participants or delivered in person. Thirty questionnaires were mailed. Twenty-one participants responded with completed questionnaires.

Step 5: Collecting the Data from the Pilot Study

All mailings included a self-addressed stamped envelope (SASE) for return, and confidentiality was assured to the survey participants in a cover letter. The cover letter also included the researcher's explanation to the participants of the importance of the study to the improvement of advocacy on behalf of children (see Appendix G). Participants were asked to complete and return the pilot study questionnaire one month from the date of their receipt of these documents. Two follow-up letters were sent at 2 week intervals over a 2 month period to all persons who had not completed and returned the pilot study survey questionnaire.

Step 6: Analysis of the Pilot Study Data

The instrument was a survey questionnaire, composed of 54 closed-ended and 2 mixed closed-ended/open-ended items. The pilot study questionnaire also contained 4 demographic items. The closed-ended questions were Likert-scale questions (Likert, 1932). Responses to the pilot study were analyzed. The answers were reviewed to determine how many participants responded to each item and how many items may have been skipped or given multiple answers. Other indications that questions may not have been clear, such as information written in the margins to qualify answers, were reviewed. Data from the pilot study were used for preliminary reliability analysis and instrument modifications. Suggestions made by the pilot study participants were considered. Items were deleted or revised as necessary to best improve the final version of the survey to be administered.

The Advocacy Definition Items: Research Question One

Items 1 through 7, 27, 28, 55, and 56 are the advocacy definition items.

Items 1, 2, 4, and 6. These items received no comments and no changes were made.

Item 3. The original text of Item 3 stated, "Speaking up, to be effective as advocacy, must be persuasive." It received comments from 3 participants that indicated it needed to be reworded. It was reworded to read, "To be effective as advocacy, speaking up must be persuasive."

Item 5. The original text of Item 5 stated, "Advocacy includes persuasion through the use of emotion." It received a comment from one participant who expressed trouble with understanding the meaning of "emotion." It was reworded to read: "Advocacy includes persuasion through the use of caring emotion."

Item 7. This item elicited a comment from one participant who thought the item was too long, and from another who did not like the justification on the right margin of the item's text. However, no changes were made, because the researcher could not see how the item could be shortened and maintain the necessary meaning, and no other negative comments were received about the item length or the right margin justification.

Items 27 and 28. These items elicited comments from one participant who wanted the word "primary" inserted in front of the word ethical in Item 27, and the word "secondary" in front of the word ethical in Item 28. No changes were made, because participants could express such distinctions through the Likert–scale rankings that they assigned to these items.

Items 55 and 56. These items, which combined closed-ended and open-ended items, elicited no responses directed at changing the items, with the one exception that some participants had difficulty understanding what was meant by the word, "emotion," in the definition. As was done for Item 5, the word, "caring," was added to the word, "emotion," to clarify the intent of the usage of the term.

The Advocacy Preparation Items: Research Question Two

Items 8, 9, 14, 34, 45, 46, 47, 52, 53, and 54 are the advocacy preparation items.

Items 8, 9, 14, 34, 45, 46, and 47. These items received no comments and no changes were made.

Item 52. This item elicited a comment from one participant who indicated that she possessed advocacy skills when she became a school psychologist, and

48

from another who said she could not remember. No changes were made to the item.

Item 53. This item elicited one comment from one participant who said she sought out education in advocacy. No changes were made.

Item 54. This item elicited one response from a participant who wrote, "I used to think so," referencing the item's query of whether the respondent had a good understanding of what it meant to be a school psychologist advocate. No changes were made.

The Advocacy Circumstances Items:
Research Question Three, Part 1

Items 10, 11, 12, 13, 15, 16, 17, 18, 32, 33, 36, 37, 38, 39, 40, 41, 42, 43, and 44 are the advocacy circumstances items.

Items 13, 18, 33, 38, 39, and 41. These six items received no comments and no changes were made.

Item 10. This item elicited a comment from one participant, but the comment anticipated the circumstance that school psychologists may have more than one client, which was addressed in later items in the questionnaire. No changes were made.

Item 11. This item elicited one comment from a participant who wanted the phrase, "practicing in the schools," added after "school psychologist." No changes were made. The researcher determined that the item was clear enough, and that a school psychologist not practicing in the schools might have other clients in the schools other than students. Another participant's comment anticipated later questionnaire items that addressed the circumstance of school psychologists having more than one client. Therefore, no changes were made.

Item 12. This item elicited one comment from one participant who wanted to add the phrase, "as necessary or as appropriate," to the item. However, the researcher made no changes in the item, as he determined that the item presumed that a school psychologist's concerns should be communicated as necessary or appropriate.

Item 15. This item elicited one comment from a participant who did not agree with the item, but queried whether school systems, in addition to school psychologists, could also be advocates for students. No changes were made to the item.

Item 16. This item elicited one comment from a participant who wanted to add a clause indicating that school psychologists should impact effective change. No change was made to this item, because no other comments were received for this item, and the researcher determined that impacting effective change would be subsumed in the advocacy role of school psychologists.

Item 17. This item elicited one comment from a participant who did not like the word "advocate" in the item. Another participant wanted to add the phrase, "in a non-adversarial manner," onto the end of the item. However, this item, like other items on the questionnaire, was designed to force the participants to make choices about advocacy. If participants did not like the concept of what they perceived to be advocacy, or perceived to be adversarial, there were items on the questionnaire which allowed them to express their dislike. Therefore, no changes were made.

Item 32. This item elicited one comment from a participant who expressed a desire to "problem solve" rather than be adversarial. However, this distinction was not germane to the item and no changes were made.

Items 36 and 37. These items elicited a comment from one participant who did not like what the participant perceived as making the administrator, in the participant's words, "the bad guy." However, Jacob-Timm's (1999) research shows that such conflicts do occur. Another participant questioned whether school psychologists made diagnoses. No changes were made to these items.

Item 40. This item elicited a response from one participant who, while understanding the item, wanted to avoid the forced choice requirement of the Likert scale by advocating for problem solving. No changes were made.

Item 42. This item received a comment from one participant that programs should be developed that "worked for all," and another participant opined that, even if such programs were developed, difficult students were still likely to be "driven out" of school. No changes were made to this item.

Item 43. This item elicited a comment from one participant who queried "in what way" was a school psychologist to advocate for students. However, it was not germane to eliciting a forced choice response to the item to provide in the text of the item ways in which advocacy might occur. Therefore, no changes were made to the item.

Item 44. This item elicited a comment from one participant who did not like the forced choice nature of responding. The participant instead advocated "diplomacy" to avoid a circumstance where the choice was between advocating for students and losing one's job. No changes were made to the item.

The Advocacy Capabilities Items:
Research Question Three, Part 2

Items 19, 20, 21, 26, 35, 48, 49, 50, and 51 are the advocacy capabilities items.

Items 19, 20, 21, and 26. These items originally began with the words "In order." One participant suggested deleting these opening words from each of these items. These opening words were deleted from each of these items.

Item 26. This item elicited a response from one participant who did not like the word "adversarial." No changes were made, because the item was intended to measure the degree to which participants agreed or disagreed with whether being adversarial with parents was necessary for effective advocacy.

Items 35, 48, 50, and 51. These items received no comments and no changes were made.

Item 49. This item elicited one comment from one participant, and only one participant, who queried what "others" meant. No changes were made to the item, because it was determined that a precise definition of "others" was not necessary in order to respond to the item.

The Advocacy Barriers/Enablers Items:
Research Question Three, Part 3

Items 22, 23, 24, 25, 29, 30, and 31 are the advocacy barriers/enablers

items.

Items 29, 30, and 31. These three items received no comments and no

changes were made.

Item 22. This item elicited a response from one participant who wrote that

this was a hard item to answer. No changes were made.

Item 23. This item received a response from one participant who wanted to

avoid the forced choice nature of the item by writing "depends on the situation"

and "maybe try to problem solve a win-win." No changes were made.

Item 24. This item elicited a comment from one participant who wrote that

advocating for the student with the strongest legal rights would "avoid suits."

Another participant, the only other participant commenting on this item, queried

whether the strongest legal rights meant the strongest legal representation. No

changes were made.

Item 25. This item elicited a comment from one participant stating how

much the participant liked the item. No changes were made.

The Demographic Items

Items 57, 58, 59, and 60. These demographic items received no comments.

However, "Hispanic" was changed to "Latino/a" and "White" to "Anglo," as had

been previously suggested by one of the school psychologist cognitive

interviewees.

Items 61 and 62. These demographic items were not included in the pilot study, but were added to the questionnaire for the study-in-chief, subsequent to the study becoming a census survey.

Step 7: Preparation of the Questionnaire for the Study-in-Chief

The questionnaire items were based upon the definition of child advocacy proposed by the researcher and discussed by the focus group, and on the subsequent clarification and revision of the survey items based upon the expert review, the cognitive interviews, and the pilot study. The instrument was a survey questionnaire composed of both closed-ended and open-ended items. The closed-ended items were Likert-scale questions. There were 56 Likert-scale items, with items 55 and 56 also being open-ended items. Demographic data collected were gender, ethnicity, years of practice, practice locale, type of practice, and professional role. Years of practice were 0-5, 6-10, and 11 or more. Locale was defined as *rural, urban, suburban, not applicable, or mixed*; the latter meaning two or more specified locales of practice within the total years of practice. Type of practice was defined as *public, private, or not applicable.* Professional role was defined as *student, practitioner, supervisor, teacher, administrator, retired, or other.* Appropriate *multiple* categories were added when data were compiled.

Step 8: Administration of the Study-in-Chief Questionnaire

A census survey design was used. A survey design was selected because the primary intent was to collect information from a population in order to describe the views of the population (school psychologists) about the ethical

54

principle of advocacy. No other research design would have been as effective in obtaining the self-report views of school psychologists about the ethic of advocacy. This is the primary benefit of the survey design. Its primary limitation is that the information it provides is largely restricted to the self-report views it seeks. A cross-sectional survey design, as opposed to a longitudinal design, was chosen because the researcher was primarily interested in assessing the views he was researching as they existed at the time of his survey administration, and not how they might, or might not, change over time.

The survey population was the membership of Colorado Society of School Psychologists (CSSP). A mailing list of the CSSP membership was supplied to the researcher in the spring of 2006, by the then president of CSSP, at the time of the pilot study, and was subsequently used in preparation for the study-in-chief. A total of 626 CSSP listed members were mailed questionnaires in August of 2006.

Step 9: Collecting the Data from the
Study-in-Chief Questionnaire

All mailings included a self-addressed and stamped envelope (SASE) for return, and confidentiality was assured to the survey participants in the cover letter. Persons mailed the survey questionnaire received a $3.00 incentive coupon for the purchase of coffee, to promote the completion and return of the questionnaire by a deadline date. The cover letter also included the researcher's explanation to the participants of the importance of the study to the improvement of advocacy on behalf of children (see Appendix H). Four follow-up letters were sent at 2-week intervals, over a 2-month period, to all persons who had not completed and returned the survey questionnaire (see Appendix I). Data collection ended approximately 2 weeks after the final follow-up letter was sent.

Step 10: Data Analysis of the Study-in-Chief Questionnaire

Having collected and analyzed the data collected during the previous steps of the study from the focus group, expert panel, cognitive interviews, and pilot study, the data collected from the study-in-chief were analyzed. This analysis, as supplemented by the analysis of the data collected during the previous steps of the study, is provided in Chapter IV.

Closed-end question Likert-scale responses were tabulated according to percentage of responses collected from the group as a whole, and according to gender, ethnicity, years of practice, locale of practice, and professional role. The total size of the census survey and the percentage of returns, including missing values, is reported. Results are presented in text and in tables.

Open-ended survey question responses were content analyzed. This was done by development and analysis of key words, as identified by the researcher from his reading of the closed-ended and open-ended survey questionnaire responses.

CHAPTER IV. RESULTS

The study of advocacy by school psychologists used a census survey of members of the Colorado Society of School Psychologists (CSSP). The results of the data gathered from this survey are presented in this chapter. Participation rates are presented first, followed by a presentation of results that address the research questions.

Response Rate

Using a mailing list of the CSSP membership, provided to the researcher in the spring of 2006 by the then president of CSSP, 626 survey questionnaires were mailed to CSSP members. Of the 626 surveys mailed, 354 were returned, yielding a response rate of 56%, after four follow-up reminder mailings, sent at 2-week intervals over a period of 2 months. However, two returned questionnaires were eliminated, because they had 35 and 47 missing values, respectively. Five more questionnaires were eliminated because two of the respondents were clinical psychologists, and three more were social workers. This left a total of 347 useable questionnaires, or 55%.

Results for Research Questions

Research Question One

*Do experts in school psychology, and practicing school psychologists,
agree or disagree with the definition of
advocacy presented by the researcher, and what changes,
if any, would they make to that definition?*

All of the focus group experts agreed that school psychologists should be advocates for all students, not just students with disabilities, and that ethical character was important, but perhaps needed better definition. All of the focus group participants also agreed with one focus group participant who stated, as condensed by the researcher,

> I think what you're trying to do, define advocacy, is tremendous. I mean, it's needed, it's, it's critical, that we, what we bring to the understanding. When somebody I think was saying earlier that she wasn't trained in advocacy, in the program. It's because we didn't know what it was. It wasn't defined. So, I think, number one, you're going in the right direction with it.

Survey questionnaire Items 1 through 7, and Items 27 and 28, contain the components of the definition proposed by the researcher on page 5 of the questionnaire. The survey respondents were also asked to respond to this definition in Items 55 and 56 of the questionnaire, which are both closed-ended and open-ended items. Table 1 presents the distribution of responses to advocacy definition items of the entire sample and to *agree/strongly agree* for the subsample of practitioners.

Table 1

Percent Response by Category to the Advocacy Definition Items

Item	Total Sample[a]					Practitioners [b]
	SD	D	N	A	SA	A/SA
1. Advocacy obligation	.3	.0	.3	13.8	85.6	12.1/87.9
2. Speak up	.0	.3	1.7	17.6	80.3	17.0/82.1
3. Persuasive	.3	3.8	12.7	51.7	31.5	52.5/33.2

58

Table 1 (continued).

Percent Response by Category to the Advocacy Definition Items

Item	Total Sample[a]					Practitioners [b]
	SD	D	N	A	SA	A/SA
4. Persuasive logic	.0	1.2	12.7	51.6	34.6	55.4/33.5
5. Persuasive emotion	.0	1.7	15.0	52.6	30.6	54.0/31.3
6. Persuasive ethical	.0	.9	8.1	35.5	55.5	33.6/57.8
7. FAPE/IDEA/ LRE	.0	.6	3.0	33.3	63.1	33.3/63.8
27. FAPE/IDEA/ LRE	.3	.0	.9	23.1	75.8	21.9/76.8
28. FAPE/LRE - all stud.	.6	1.4	4.0	25.6	68.3	27.2/67.4
55. Advocacy Def. - IDEA stud.	1.5	3.2	12.0	54.1	29.2	55.2/30.3
56. Advocacy Def. - all stud.	2.4	3.9	14.2	45.5	33.9	46.9/34.3

Note. Responses are shown in percentages. Stud. = student(s); FAPE = free appropriate public education; IDEA = Individuals With Disabilities Education Act; LRE = least restrictive environment; def. = definition.
[a] N = 330 – 347, which represents the number-range of participants in the total sample who responded to the items in Table 1.
[b] N = 213 – 224, which represents the number-range of practitioner participants who responded to the items in Table 1.

Almost all of the survey participants responding either agreed or strongly agreed with questionnaire Item 1, that school psychologists have an ethical obligation to be advocates for students. All of those responding to this item who identified their professional roles primarily as practitioners either agreed or strongly agreed with this item. Almost all of the survey participants also either agreed or strongly agreed with questionnaire Item 2, that school psychologists have an ethical obligation to speak up on behalf of students. Almost all of those responding to this item who identified their professional roles primarily as practitioners either agreed or strongly agreed with this item.

The strength of these positive majorities drops, however (to about 85%), for questionnaire Item 3, that to be effective as advocacy speaking up must be persuasive. Only about 3 out of every 10 survey participants strongly agreed.

Similarly, approximately 8 to 9 out of every 10 of all the survey participants responding either agreed or strongly agreed with questionnaire Item 4, that advocacy includes persuasion through the use of logic, and Item 5, that advocacy includes persuasion through the use of caring emotion. Only about one third of the survey participants strongly agreed, and only about one third of the practitioner participants strongly agreed.

The positive majority of response increases to approximately 9 out of every 10 survey participants responding who either agreed or strongly agreed with questionnaire Item 6, that advocacy includes persuasion by demonstrating appropriate ethical character.

An even higher number of all the survey participants responding either agreed or strongly agreed with questionnaire Item 7, that advocacy by school psychologists for students with disabilities requires the creation of IEPs that provide a FAPE in the LRE. Almost all of the survey participants responding either agreed or strongly agreed with questionnaire Item 27, which was a shorter restatement of questionnaire Item 7 that school psychologists have an ethical obligation to advocate for a FAPE for students with disabilities.

The strength of this positive majority was slightly decreased to approximately 9 out of every 10 of all the survey participants responding, who either agreed or strongly agreed with questionnaire Item 28, which was a restatement of Items 7 and 27, with the qualification that Item 28 stated that school psychologists have an ethical obligation to advocate for a FAPE for all students, not just students with disabilities.

About 8 out of every 10 of all the survey participants responding either agreed or strongly agreed with survey questionnaire Item 55, which stated that the researcher's proposed definition of advocacy is appropriate for IDEA students and with Item 56, which stated that the researcher's proposed definition of advocacy is appropriate for all students. However, only about 3 out of every 10 survey participants strongly agreed.

Summary

Thus, as can be seen from Table 1, the responses to individual questionnaire Items 1, 2, 3, 4, 5, 6, 7, 27, and 28, which state the components of the researcher's proposed definition of advocacy for school psychologists (provided in whole on page 7 of the questionnaire in Appendix K), showed majorities in agreement with the researcher's proposed definition. However, the strength of the majorities in response to questionnaire Items 3, 4, 5, and, to a lesser extent, Item 6, were not as great as the majorities in response to the other questionnaire items. The responses of the survey participants to questionnaire

Items 55 and 56, as can also be seen from Table 1, produced majorities similar to those produced for questionnaire Items 3, 4, and 5.

The Written Comments for Items 55 and 56

A total of 229, or 65%, of all survey participants responding, offered some written comment to questionnaire Items 55 or 56, which asked participants to provide a Likert-scale response and an open-ended response to the researcher's proposed definition of advocacy for school psychologists. Questionnaire Item 55 posited the proposed definition for IDEA students. Questionnaire Item 56 posited the proposed definition for all students.

The researcher identified key words in the responses to open-ended Items 55 and 56. These key words were identified from the definition of advocacy proposed by the researcher in Items 55 and 56, and in Likert-scale Items 1, 2, 3, 4, 5, 6, 27, and 28. The key words, or some derivative of them, included persuade, caring emotion, logic, ethical character, and speak up. These key words, or some derivative of them, were used in response to open-ended Items 55 or 56 by 87, or 38%, of the participants who responded with open-ended written comments to these items. Of these participants, 11, or 13%, disagreed or strongly disagreed with the definition of advocacy proposed by the researcher; 19, or 22%, were neutral; and 57, or 65%, agreed or strongly agreed with the researcher's proposed definition for advocacy.

The researcher then further examined these responses by 87 of the participants to determine which participants were critical of, or expressed some concern about the key words, or some derivative of them, identified for analysis by the researcher: persuade, caring emotion, logic, ethical character, and speak up. There were 37 such responses.

No participant who strongly agreed with the researcher's proposed definition of advocacy was critical of any of the key words. Of those participants who agreed with the researcher's proposed definition, as indicated by their choice of a Likert response 4 to either Item 55 or 56, and who provided some written comment containing a key word or key word derivative, 19 were critical of one or more of the key words identified by the researcher. Specifically, 8 were critical of the usage of "ethical character" (5 of these were practitioners); 8 were critical of the usage of "persuade" (4 of these were practitioners); 2 were critical of the usage of "caring emotion" (1 of these was a practitioner), and 1, a practitioner, was critical of the usage of "speak up."

Of those participants who indicated that they were neutral to the researcher's proposed definition, as indicated by their choice of a Likert response 3 to either Item 55 or 56, and who provided some written comment containing a key word or key word derivative, 9 were critical of one or more of the identified key words. Specifically, 3 were critical of the usage of "ethical character" (2 of these were practitioners); 5 were critical of the usage of "persuade" (2 of these were practitioners), and 1, a practitioner, was critical of the usage of "logic."

Of those participants who indicated that they disagreed or strongly disagreed with the researcher's proposed definition, as indicated by their choice of a Likert response 1 or 2 to either Item 55 or 56, and who provided some written comment containing a key word or key word derivative, 9 were critical of one or more of the key words identified by the researcher. Specifically, 7 were critical of the usage of "ethical character" (5 of these were practitioners); 2 (1 of whom was a practitioner) were critical of the usage of "persuade."

Although the number of these critical comments was small, the researcher found them to be significant, because the concerns expressed about the usage of "ethical character" and "persuade" are consistent with the lower percentages of agreement that were obtained for Likert-scale Items 3, 4, 5, and to a lesser extent, Item 6, all of which contain components of the researcher's proposed definition of advocacy. The usage of "ethical character" was also of concern to the focus group. The usage of a derivative of "persuade" is a common component of Likert-scale Items 3, 4, 5, and 6; and "ethical character" is a component of Item 6. Also, the written concerns expressed in Items 55 and 56, in response to the researcher's proposed definition of advocacy, about the usage of "ethical character" and "persuade," were consistent whether the participant gave the item a Likert-scale rating of a 4, 3, 2, or 1.

Four of these participants, who agreed with the researcher's proposed definition of advocacy, nevertheless stated that "ethical character" needed to be better defined. Two other participants, who agreed with the researcher's proposed definition, questioned whether "ethical character" was the most fundamental component of that definition, as the researcher claimed.

One of the participants who gave the researcher's proposed definition of advocacy a neutral ranking stated, "I've seen too many school psychs, under the mantle of 'ethical advocacy,' become crusaders for a cause that may ultimately be detrimental to many students." Another participant, who gave the proposed definition a neutral ranking, thought "ethical character" needed to be better defined; and another wanted to know how "ethical character" was going to be measured.

Three of the participants who disagreed with the researcher's proposed definition of advocacy also indicated that "ethical character" needed to be better defined. Another participant who disagreed with the researcher's proposed definition emphasized that school psychologists had ethical obligations to their school district employers. Another participant who disagreed with the researcher's proposed definition stated, "I disagree with the statement that 'the most fundamental is ethical character.' You can have great ethical character and be a lousy advocate." Another who disagreed stated, "I know a lot of 'good' 'ethical' people with the best of intentions who have and continue to harm children while they think they are helping." Another who disagreed also thought that there was too much emphasis in the definition on ethics.

The usage of "persuade" was criticized by one participant who otherwise agreed with the researcher's proposed definition of advocacy. This participant stated, "The word 'persuade' tends to have an aura of manipulation associated with it. I would change 'persuade' to 'educate.'" Another participant who

65

otherwise agreed with the researcher's proposed definition stated, "I am not trying to persuade others to follow my lead, but rather state the facts in a way that incorporates all knowledge gathered from those involved." Similarly, another participant who otherwise agreed with the researcher's proposed definition stated, "While, indeed, successful advocacy is often persuasive, the definition slightly implies that one's advocacy should out-persuade another's perspective." Another participant who agreed with the researcher's proposed definition nonetheless objected to the word, persuade, because it connoted selling. Another participant who agreed with the researcher's proposed definition did not like what the participant saw as the connotation of persuasion with argumentation. Another who agreed with the proposed definition thought "persuasion" needed to be better defined.

Of those who were neutral to the researcher's proposed definition of advocacy, one participant stated, "Persuasive discussion in not dialogue or open debate by the team involved with one child/student and their family." Another such participant suggested the use of the word effective, rather than persuasive. Another stated, "I'm not crazy about the word 'persuade,' because it sounds covert." Another participant who gave the definition a neutral ranking was concerned with the usage of the word persuasive because "IDEA students and their parents may be in a situation emotionally or cognitively where they could be easily swayed." Another thought "persuasive" needed to be better defined.

Of the two participants who disagreed with the use of the word persuasion in the researcher's proposed definition of advocacy, one stated that speaking up for a student did not necessarily require persuasion, which this participant connoted with being adversarial. The other participant queried, "Why does advocacy have to include persuasion?"

Research Question Two
How prepared do experts in school psychology, and practicing
school psychologists, believe school psychologists
are to fulfill their ethical obligation to advocate
for individual students with disabilities?

Focus group school psychologist experts had already indicated that they thought advocacy was an appropriate ethical role for school psychologists. They had also indicated that school psychologists could be better prepared for this practice of advocacy, and thus the practice of advocacy could be improved, through the teaching of ethics and advocacy and through better mentoring and supervision of school psychologists. Survey participants, including practicing school psychologists, agreed. Table 2 presents the distribution of responses to advocacy preparation items of the entire sample and to *agree/strongly agree* for the subsample of practitioners.

67

Table 2

Percent Response by Category to the Advocacy Preparation Items

Item	Total Sample[a]					Practitoners[b]
	SD	D	N	A	SA	A/SA
8. Advocates for students	.0	.3	.9	27.8	71.0	27.7/71.4
9. Advocates for students with disabilities	.0	.3	.9	26.5	72.3	25.9/73.9
14. Ethics education	.0	.0	.3	20.2	79.5	20.2/79.4
34. Advocacy education	.0	.3	.3	30.9	68.5	33.2/65.9
45. S.D.sch.psych.- effective advoc.	.3	.0	2.6	39.1	58.0	40.1/56.3
46. S.D.sch.psych.- ethical advoc.	.3	.6	.9	36.4	61.8	37.7/60.1
47. S.D.sch.psych. vs. other	.0	8.1	16.2	33.0	42.6	33.6/42.2
52. Sufficient ed.	6.7	25.7	24.6	35.1	7.9	36.9/08.1
53. Ongoing ed.	7.7	35.7	29.8	22.4	4.4	21.6/03.2
54. Advocacy understanding	1.2	2.6	15.1	55.1	26.1	54.5/27.0

Note. Responses are shown in percentages. S.D. = school district; sch. = school; psych. = psychologist; advoc. = advocate; ed. = education.
[a] N = 339 – 346, which represents the number-range of participants in the total sample who responded to the items in Table 2.
[b] N = 222 – 231, which represents the number-range of practitioner participants who responded to the items in Table 2.

Almost all of the survey participants responding to questionnaire Item 8 agreed or strongly agreed with the statement that they were advocates for students. Almost all of those responding to this item who identified their

68

professional roles primarily as school psychologist practitioners either agreed or strongly agreed. More specifically, responding to questionnaire Item 9, almost all of the survey participants agreed or strongly agreed with the statement that they were advocates for students with disabilities.

Almost all of the survey participants responding to questionnaire Item 14 also agreed or strongly agreed with the statement that professional education in school psychology should include ethics education. Similarly, Item 34 garnered strong agreement with the statement that school psychologists should be educated about how to be successful advocates; as did Item 45, that school psychologists employed by school districts can be effective advocates for students; and Item 46, that school psychologists employed by school districts can be ethical advocates for students.

However, of those survey participants responding to questionnaire Item 47, only about three quarters agreed or strongly agreed with the statement that school psychologists employed by school districts can be as effective in their advocacy as school psychologists who are employed in different settings. Only about 4 out of every 10 of those survey participants responding to questionnaire Item 52 agreed or strongly agreed with the statement that they received sufficient education in advocacy as a part of their professional education in school psychology. Only about one quarter of those survey participants responding to questionnaire Item 53 agreed or strongly agreed with the statement that they received sufficient ongoing education in advocacy.

About 8 out of every 10 of those survey participants responding to questionnaire Item 54 agreed or strongly agreed with the statement that they had a good understanding of what it meant to be a school psychologist advocate.

Summary

Thus, as can be seen from Table 2, strong majorities of survey participants, including school psychologist practitioners, indicated that (a) they were advocates for students, (b) they were advocates for students with disabilities, (c) professional education in school psychology should include ethics education, (d) school psychologists should be educated about how to be successful advocates, (e) school psychologists employed by school districts can be effective advocates for students, and (f) school psychologists employed by school districts can be ethical advocates for students.

However, when survey participants, including practitioners, were queried about whether they have received, and are receiving, sufficient education in advocacy, these majorities of agreement disappeared. Indeed, 3 out of every 10 of all survey participants responding disagreed or strongly disagreed that they had received sufficient education in advocacy. And, about 4 out of every 10 of all survey participants responding disagreed or strongly disagreed with the statement that they received sufficient ongoing education in advocacy. Less than half of the practitioner participants responding agreed or strongly agreed that they had received sufficient education in advocacy, and less than one quarter agreed or strongly agreed that they received sufficient ongoing education in advocacy.

70

Majorities, including practitioners, did agree that they thought school

psychologists employed in public schools could be as effective in their advocacy

as school psychologists employed in other settings, and that they had a good

understanding of what it meant to be a school psychologist advocate. However,

these majorities of agreement were not as strong as the majorities of agreement

for Items 8, 9, 14, 34, 45, and 46, as can also be seen from Table 2.

Research Question Three

As perceived by practicing school psychologists, and by school psychology experts, (a) what are the circumstances within which the ethical obligation for advocacy for individual students with disabilities manifests itself within the practice of school psychology, (b) what are the capabilities necessary for school psychologists to be effective advocates for individual students with disabilities, and (c) what are barriers to, and enablers of, effective advocacy by school psychologists on behalf of individual students with disabilities?

Part 1. The Advocacy Circumstances Items

What are the circumstances within which the ethical obligation for advocacy for students with disabilities manifests itself within the practice of school psychology?

One focus group expert, in responding to the researcher's focus group

prompt question asking how the practice of advocacy could be improved, told

what she labeled a "war story" from early in her school psychology practice.

Today, the student in this war story might, or might not, depending upon the

development of further facts, have been labeled a student with a disability. This

war story exemplified a circumstance within which an ethical obligation to be an

advocate manifested itself, and how a school psychologist overcame a barrier and

was able to capably handle what she perceived to be her advocacy obligation.

71

The school psychologist began by stating that in being an advocate and in honoring a school district employer's needs, there is a need to know the laws well, your ethical and professional responsibilities well, and what your role is and is not. She told her story, as condensed by the researcher, as follows:

> When I was new to school psychology I had an office next to the Assistant Principal. His way of disciplining was to just yell at the kids. You know, those walls are so paper thin, and you just have to listen and listen and listen. And then, they had a rule that, that he had a paddle, like a paddle, like a paddle like a sorority or a fraternity paddle, and if the parents agreed, he could bend the kid over and slap him on the butt a few times, versus give him a detention, or something like that. And I, I just was horrified. So that was a real ethical dilemma, in terms of, what's my role going to be and how much can I advocate for these children around this, and how humiliating. So the rule was, again talking about the rules, the rule was that, they had to have a witness, in the room, in order to paddle them. They would literally bend over, and count 3 slaps, I guess, depending on … I refused to witness. That was my first thing. I mean, I knew that much, that I did not have to witness something like this, and I refused to do that. And then I talked to my supervisors, and shared my concerns with it. I basically shared policy from our national association, against corporal punishment, and then, copied information for the administrators and sent it around to the school. Now, and, I did my best to have a relationship with that administrator. In a way that I might be influential around. So there you have a, a ethical dilemma, that's a perspective.

Another focus group participant observed that a school psychologist might have a difficult time staying employed in such a circumstance. The school psychologist telling the story then continued:

> At that point, it almost didn't matter to me that much. I mean it was beyond that for me. It was a matter of, I could not, it was beyond tolerance. I have to say, I did it quietly. I put out my little corporal punishment newspapers, and newsletters, and tried to be a team member with that Assistant Principal. And, all I know is that it didn't happen as much when I was around. And if that helped, you know, come up with other ways of, especially, if we want to talk about the IEP kids, but it didn't matter, if they were kids within special education or not. I was

72

there. What other opportunities, what other ways could we manage, you know, punishment, besides that. I keep hearing advocacy, and then I think rules, and having been an administrator, having been a school psychologist, you know, that tightrope is, you know, a real tough one to walk.

The circumstances of advocacy were also addressed by the survey. Table 3 presents the distribution of responses to advocacy circumstances items of the entire sample and to *agree/strongly agree* for the subsample of practitioners.

Table 3

Percent Response by Category to the Advocacy Circumstances Items

Item	Total Sample[a]					Practitioners[b]
	SD	D	N	A	SA	A/SA
10. Stud.as pri.client	1.2	1.8	7.3	36.8	52.9	35.9/54.3
11. Stud.as pri.obligation	1.2	2.6	14.9	37.4	43.9	37.4/45.0
12. Communicate concerns	.0	.0	2.9	33.8	63.3	33.0/64.3
13. Stud.as top priority	.0	2.6	5.8	42.9	48.7	41.4/50.5
15. Stud.vs.system	1.2	2.9	12.2	38.3	45.5	41.9/43.7
16. Pri. role as advocate	.9	5.5	15.7	39.2	38.7	38.5/39.4
17. Advoc.for serv.	.3	1.7	8.4	43.9	45.6	44.6/44.6
18. Advoc. for ed. change	0	.3	5.2	44.1	50.4	45.9/50.0
32. Student's best interests	.6	.9	9.0	44.8	44.8	47.1/42.6
33. Student as pri. client	.6	1.2	11.2	42.4	44.7	46.0/42.0
36. Diagnosis	.9	2.3	7.0	31.7	58.1	30.8/60.2
37. Cost	1.7	15.7	25.0	35.2	22.4	37.2/22.4

Table 3 (continued).

The Advocacy Circumstances Items

Item	Total Sample[a]					Practitioners[b]
	SD	D	N	A	SA	A/SA
38. Stud. as IDEA qual.	52.2	34.0	9.0	2.6	2.0	1.1/02.2
39. Stud.not qual.	61.0	28.6	7.8	1.7	.9	1.3/00.9
40. Serv.available	2.0	8.5	21.9	48.1	19.5	51.1/17.9
41. Private placem.	5.3	18.2	36.4	31.7	8.5	33.9/06.8
42. Approp.programs	.0	1.4	9.5	55.5	33.5	55.6/33.2
43. Poor teaching	.0	1.2	6.1	45.3	47.4	44.3/48.4
44. Job jeopardy	1.8	9.8	33.1	42.0	13.3	43.1/12.8

Note. Responses are shown in percentages. Stud. = student; pri. = primary; advoc. = advocate; serv. = services; ed. = education; qual. = qualified; placem. – placement; approp. = appropriate.
[a]N = 338 – 346, which represents the number-range of participants in the total sample who responded to the items in Table 3.
[b]N = 218 – 224, which represents the number-range of practitioner participants who responded to the items in Table 3.

Slightly less than 9 out of every 10 of all the survey participants responding to questionnaire Item 10, which states that a school psychologist's primary clients are students, agreed or strongly agreed. About 8 out of every 10 of all the survey participants responding to questionnaire Item 11 which states that school psychologists have a primary obligation to their student clients when conflicts exist with other clients agreed or strongly agreed. All but 10 of all the survey participants responding to questionnaire Item 12, which states that school psychologists should communicate their concerns for protecting the rights and welfare of students to school administration and staff, agreed or strongly agreed.

74

Approximately 9 out of every 10 of all the survey participants responding to questionnaire Item 13, which states that the rights and welfare of students should be the top priority in determining services for students, agreed or strongly agreed. Approximately 8 out of every 10 of all the survey participants responding to questionnaire Item 15, which states that the primary client of a school psychologist is the student not the school system, agreed or strongly agreed.

Somewhat less than 8 out of every 10 of all the survey participants responding to questionnaire Item 16, which states that the primary role of a school psychologist is to be an advocate for students, agreed or strongly agreed. Slightly less than 9 out of every 10 of all the survey participants responding to questionnaire Item 17, which states that school psychologists should advocate to help students get the educational services they need, even if school districts are reluctant to provide those services, agreed or strongly agreed. More than 9 out of every 10 of all the survey participants responding to questionnaire Item 18, which states that a school psychologist should advocate for educational change in order to meet the needs of all students, agreed or strongly agreed.

Slightly less than 9 out of every 10 of all the survey participants responding to questionnaire Item 32, which states that if conflicts of interest between a school psychologist's clients are present the school psychologist should support conclusions that are in the best interests of the student client, agreed or strongly agreed. Somewhat less than 9 out of every 10 of all the survey participants responding to questionnaire Item 33, which states that when a school

75

psychologist is confronted with conflicts between client groups the primary client is considered to be the student, agreed or strongly agreed. Slightly less than 9 out of every 10 of all the survey participants responding to questionnaire Item 36, which states that a school psychologist should provide the diagnosis she/he thinks is accurate even if a school administrator disagrees, agreed or strongly agreed.

Somewhat less than 6 out of every 10 of all the survey participants responding to questionnaire Item 37, which states that a school psychologist should recommend what s/he thinks is appropriate for a student regardless of cost, agreed or strongly agreed. Only a total of 16, or 4.6%, of all the survey participants responding to questionnaire Item 38, which states that a school psychologist should find a student qualified for IDEA services, if requested by a school administrator to do so, agreed or strongly agreed.

Only a total of 9, or 2.6%, of all the survey participants responding to questionnaire Item 39, which states that a school psychologist should find a student not qualified for IDEA services, if requested by a school administrator to do so, agreed or strongly agreed. Somewhat less than 7 out of every 10 of all the survey participants responding to questionnaire Item 40, which states that a school psychologist should recommend what she/he believes are needed services for a student, regardless of whether the employing school district had those services available, agreed or strongly agreed. Approximately 4 out of every 10 of all the survey participants responding to questionnaire Item 41, which states that a school psychologist advocate should recommend what she/he believes is a needed private placement for a student regardless of cost, agreed or strongly agreed. Slightly less than 9 out of every 10 of all the survey participants responding to questionnaire Item 42, which states that a school psychologist advocate should attempt to develop appropriate programs for difficult students even if administrators or other school staff do not want the students in school, agreed or strongly agreed.

Somewhat more than 9 out of every 10 of all the survey participants responding to questionnaire Item 43, which states that a school psychologist should advocate for students who are not receiving an appropriate education because of poor teaching practices, agreed or strongly agreed. Somewhat more than half of all the survey participants responding to questionnaire Item 44, which states that a school psychologist should advocate for students who are not receiving an appropriate education, even if doing so is likely to cost the school psychologist his/her job, agreed or strongly agreed.

Summary

In the Advocacy section of the NASP *Principles for Professional Ethics* (2000), these statements are made:

> When the school psychologist is confronted with conflicts between client groups, the primary client is considered to be the child….If conflicts of interest between clients are present, the school psychologist supports conclusions that are in the best interests of the child….School psychologists' concerns for protecting the rights and welfare of children are communicated to the school administration and staff as the top priority in determining services (pp. 25-26).

These are circumstances within which the ethical obligation for advocacy for individual students with disabilities, and for all students, manifests itself.

77

Questionnaire Items 10, 11, 12, 13, 15, 32, and 33 are composed of paraphrases of this language. As evidenced by survey participants' responses to these questionnaire items, majorities of Colorado Society of School Psychologists (CSSP) members, including practicing school psychologists, agree with these NASP ethical admonitions.

However, as can be seen from Table 3, with the exception of participant responses to questionnaire Items 12 and 13, which stated, respectively, that school psychologists should communicate their concerns for protecting the rights and welfare of students to school administration and staff, and the rights and welfare of students should be the top priority in determining services for students, none of these questionnaire items obtained agreement majorities of at least 90% from all survey participants. Questionnaire Item 10, which stated that a school psychologist's primary clients are students, did obtain 90.2% agreement from practitioners, with about half of the practitioners strongly agreeing. Questionnaire Item 12 obtained majorities of agreement, including practitioners, above 97%, with above 60% strong agreement. Questionnaire item 13 obtained majorities of agreement above 91%, with above 48% of all participants, and above 50% of practitioners, strongly agreeing.

What questionnaire Items 10, 11, 15, 32, and 33 have in common, is the assertion, consistent with the admonition in the NASP *Principles for Professional Ethics*, that the primary client of the school psychologist is the student, even if other clients exist. The majorities of agreement for questionnaire Items 11 and 15 were especially low.

Questionnaire Item 11 stated that, if conflicts exist between student clients and any other clients, the primary obligation of the school psychologist is to the student clients. Over 81% of all participants, and over 82% of practitioner participants, agreed; and 43.9% and 45%, respectively, strongly agreed. However, 51 participants were neutral to this statement, 9 disagreed, and 4 strongly disagreed, for a total of 64, or 18.7%. Of practitioner participants responding to this item, 30 were neutral, 8 disagreed, and 1 strongly disagreed, for a total of 39, or 17.6%.

Questionnaire Item 15 stated that the primary client of a school psychologist is the student, not the school system. Over 83% of all participants and over 85% of practitioner participants agreed, and over 45% and over 43%, respectively, strongly agreed. However, 42 participants were neutral to this statement, 10 disagreed, and 4 strongly disagreed, for a total of 56, or 16.2%. Of practitioner participants responding to this item, 26 were neutral and 6 disagreed, for a total of 32, or 14.4%

Questionnaire Items 17, 18, 42, and 43, all represent specific instances of circumstances where school psychologists can be asked to advocate for the best interests, rights, and welfare of their primary clients. All received strong majorities of agreement from responding survey participants, including school psychology practitioners. However, when this advocacy is conditioned by the cost of services, as in questionnaire Item 37; or by the school district availability of services, as in questionnaire Item 40; or by job security for the school psychologist, as in questionnaire Item 44, these majorities of agreement substantially diminish. In the case of a potentially needed private placement, Item 41, there was no majority of agreement.

Questionnaire Items 36, 38, and 39 represent circumstances where school psychologists might be in disagreement with school district administrators about appropriately determining the nature of a student's problems, including the potential need for IDEA services. Survey participants, including practitioners, overwhelmingly rejected assertions that a school psychologist's decision making as a participant in these determinations should be dictated by school district administrators. Finally, a majority of survey participants, including practitioners, agreed in responding to questionnaire Item 16, that the primary role of a school psychologist is be an advocate for students. However, these majorities of agreement, 77.9% for all survey participants, and also 77.9% for practitioners, leave substantial minorities, most of whom were neutral to this assertion.

Part 2. The Advocacy Capabilities Items

*What are the capabilities necessary for school
 psychologists to be effective advocates for
individual students with disabilities?*

Table 4 presents the distribution of responses to advocacy capabilities items of the entire sample and to *agree/strongly agree* for the subsample of practitioners.

Table 4

Percent Response by Category to the Advocacy Capabilities Items

Item	Total Sample[a]					Practitioners[b]
	SD	D	N	A	SA	A/SA
19. Adversarial with staff	5.2	14.8	22.0	44.3	13.6	48.6/13.5
26. Adversarial with parents	6.7	26.4	21.2	40.0	5.8	42.6/05.8
20. Student needs	1.5	2.9	15.2	54.2	26.2	56.1/25.8
21. Collaborate with others	.3	.3	.6	11.8	87.0	11.2/87.4
35. Resolve conflict	.0	2.0	6.6	34.3	57.1	33.9/56.7
48. Listener	.0	.0	.3	13.9	85.8	15.2/84.4
49. Other views	.0	.3	6.1	33.7	59.9	36.0/56.8
50. Consensus	.0	.3	1.4	23.1	75.1	24.2/74.4
51. Persuaded by others	.6	1.7	10.4	43.6	43.6	44.4/42.6

Note. Responses are shown in percentages. S.D. = school district; sch. = school; psych. = psychologist; advoc. = advocate; ed. = education.
[a]N = 343 – 347, which represents the number-range of participants in the total sample who responded to the items in Table 4.
[b]N = 221 – 224, which represents the number-range of practitioner participants who responded to the items in Table 4.

Approximately 6 out of every 10 of all survey participants responding to questionnaire Item 19, which states that to be effective advocates for students, school psychologists must sometimes be adversarial with other school staff, agreed or strongly agreed with the statement.

Less than half of all survey participants responding to questionnaire Item 26, which states that to be effective student advocates school psychologists must

81

sometimes be adversarial with parents, agreed or strongly agreed with the statement.

Approximately 8 out of every 10 of all survey participants responding to questionnaire Item 20, which states that to be effective advocates for students school psychologists must sometimes place the needs of students above the needs of the school system, agreed or strongly agreed with the statement.

Almost all of the survey respondents responding to questionnaire Item 21, which states that to be effective as advocates school psychologists should collaborate with others on behalf of students, agreed or strongly agreed with the statement.

Approximately 9 out of every 10 of all survey participants responding to questionnaire Item 35, which states that a school psychologist advocate attempts to resolve conflicts of interest between client groups in a manner that is mutually beneficial and protects the rights of all parties, agreed or strongly agreed.

Almost all of the survey participants responding to questionnaire Item 48, which states that a school psychologist needs to be a good listener, agreed or strongly agreed.

Somewhat more than 9 out of every 10 of all survey participants responding to questionnaire Item 49, which states that a school psychologist advocate needs to be able to help others express their views even when the school psychologist disagrees with those views, agreed or strongly agreed with the statement.

Almost all of the survey participants responding to questionnaire Item 50, which states that a school psychologist advocate needs to know how to work with teams in order to reach consensus, agreed or strongly agreed. Somewhat less than 9 out of every 10 of all survey participants responding to questionnaire Item 51, which states a school psychologist advocate should be open to being persuaded by others who are advocating on behalf of students, agreed or strongly agreed.

Summary

Thus, as can be seen from Table 4, there were strong majorities of agreement among survey participants, including practitioners, that school psychologists (a) should be collaborative, (b) should attempt to resolve conflicts between client groups in a manner that is mutually beneficial and protects the rights of all parties, (c) should be good listeners, (d) need to be able to help others express views with which the school psychologist may disagree, (e) need to be able to work with teams in order to reach consensus, and, to a somewhat lesser extent, (f) need to be open to being persuaded by others.

The majority of agreement was less strong, though still substantial, for placing the needs of the student above the needs of the school system. The majority of agreement was substantially reduced, however, when the proposition is that to be effective advocates school psychologists must sometimes be adversarial with other school staff. And, when the proposition is that to be effective advocates school psychologists must sometimes be adversarial with parents, the majority of agreement disappeared.

83

Part 3. The Advocacy Barriers/Enablers Items

What are the barriers to, and enablers of, effective advocacy by school psychologists on behalf of individual students with disabilities?

One of the attorney experts who reviewed potential questionnaire items for the survey stated that the most common ethical dilemma in special education is that resources are finite, and that resources allocated to one student often means that one or more other students will receive less resources. The attorney provided the following example, as condensed by the researcher:

> A student's parent is cross-wise with the resource teacher in an elementary school. All agree life would be much smoother if the student had a different resource teacher. The student spends about half his day in resource. There is another resource teacher in the building, but she is on a different schedule with different grade-level kids. For this student to be granted his request for a different teacher, 12 other students will have to be switched at this time of year to a different teacher. All agree it would be "better" for the one student. All agree it would be "worse" for the 12. But none of the 12 who will be disrupted have filed for due process.

Table 5 presents the distribution of responses to advocacy barriers/ enablers items of the entire sample and to *agree/strongly agree* for the subsample of practitioners.

Table 5

Percent Response by Category to the Advocacy Barriers/Enablers Items

Item	Total Sample[a]					Practitioners[b]
	SD	D	N	A	SA	A/SA
22. Stud. advocacy conflict	4.1	13.3	29.6	41.2	11.9	39.9/11.7
23. Student with greatest need	6.4	17.2	47.5	22.7	6.1	22.6/06.3

Table 5 (continued).

Percent Response by Category to the Advocacy Barriers/Enablers Items

Item	Total Sample[a]					Practitioners[b]
	SD	D	N	A	SA	A/SA
24. Student with legal rights	11.4	32.2	46.8	8.2	1.5	7.3/00.9
25. Greatest good	1.7	7.6	22.7	45.5	22.4	47.3/21.2
29. Parent as client	.9	11.8	16.4	51.3	19.6	53.1/18.8
30. Teacher as client	2.6	10.4	16.5	51.4	19.1	53.4/17.5
31. School system as client	4.3	11.6	17.7	49.3	17.1	51.1/14.8

Note. Responses are shown in percentages. Stud. = student.
[a] N = 342 – 347, which represents the number-range of participants in the total sample who responded to the items in Table 5.
[b] N = 220 – 224, which represents the number-range of practitioner participants who responded to the items in Table 5.

Only slightly more than half of all survey participants responding to questionnaire Item 22, which states that a school psychologist's advocacy for one student may sometimes conflict with the advocacy needs of one or more other students, agreed or strongly agreed. Less than 3 out of every 10 of all survey participants responding to questionnaire Item 23, which states that if a school psychologist's advocacy for one student conflicts with advocacy for one or more other students the school psychologist should advocate for the student or students with the greatest need, agreed or strongly agreed. A total of 33, less than 10%, of all survey participants responding to questionnaire Item 24, which states that if a school psychologist's advocacy conflicts with advocacy for one or more other students the school psychologist should advocate for the student or students with the strongest legal rights, agreed or strongly agreed. Somewhat less than 7 out of every 10 of all the survey participants responding to questionnaire Item 25, which states that if a school psychologist's advocacy for one student conflicts with advocacy for one or more other students, the school psychologist should advocate for an outcome that would provide the greatest good for the greatest number of students, agreed or strongly agreed. Approximately 7 out of every 10 of all the survey participants responding to questionnaire Item 29, which states that parents are a school psychologist's clients, agreed or strongly agreed. Approximately 7 out of every 10 of all the survey participants responding to questionnaire Item 30, which states that teachers are a school psychologist's clients, agreed or strongly agreed. Between 6 and 7 out of every 10 of all the survey participants responding to questionnaire Item 31, which states that school systems are a school psychologist's clients, agreed or strongly agreed.

Summary

Thus, as can be seen from Table 5, a bare majority of survey participants, including practitioners, in responding to questionnaire Item 22, thought that advocacy for one student might sometimes conflict with advocacy for one or more other students. This bare majority disappeared when survey participants were asked whether the way to resolve conflicts between student needs was to advocate for the student, or students, with the greatest needs, as was proposed in questionnaire Item 23. The percentages of agreement and disagreement for this proposition moved towards equality for all survey participants. Only 28.9% of practitioners agreed or strongly agreed that the way to resolve conflicts between student needs was to advocate for the student or students with the greatest needs.

When survey participants were asked whether conflicts between a school psychologist's advocacy for one student and one or more other students should be resolved in favor of the student with the greatest legal rights, the majorities of agreement not only disappear, they approach majorities of disagreement. Of all survey participants responding, 43.6% disagreed or strongly disagreed that legal rights should be controlling. Only 8.2% of practitioner participants responding agreed or strongly agreed that legal rights should be controlling. Majorities of agreement returned when it was proposed, as in questionnaire Item 25, that when there were conflicts in a school psychologist's advocacy between students, the conflict should be resolved by advocating for an outcome that would provide the greatest good for the greatest number of students. However, the strength of these majorities was below 70%: 67.9% for all survey participants responding and 68.5% for practitioner participants responding.

The strength of the majorities obtained for the assertions that parents and teachers are a school psychologist's clients, as was stated in questionnaire Items 29 and 30, respectively, was just above 70% for all survey participants and for practitioners. However, these majorities of agreement drop to 66.4% for all survey participants responding and to 65.9% for practitioner participants, in response to the assertion made in questionnaire Item 31, which states that school systems are a school psychologist's clients.

Findings Summary

There were strong majorities of agreement (80% or better) with the researcher's proposed definition of advocacy, with the qualifications that some concerns were expressed over the meanings of "persuasive" and "ethical character." There were strong majorities of agreement (approaching 100%) that school psychologists needed more education in advocacy in order to be better prepared as advocates. There were strong majorities of agreement (above 90%) that school psychologists should advocate for students; but survey participants also found advocating for students to be more problematic when the circumstances of this advocacy brought students into potential conflict with school district financial concerns and with job security for the school psychologist.

Survey participants were somewhat less certain (slightly less than 80%) that the primary role of a school psychologist is to be an advocate for students. Survey participants generally thought that good collaborative skills were necessary capabilities for effective advocacy by school psychologists, but they were divided over whether the capability to be adversarial with school staff and parents was necessary for effective advocacy. Responses from survey participants also indicated that conflicts between multiple clients of the school psychologist may be potential barriers to effective advocacy for students, and hence better resolution of such conflicts might enable better advocacy for students.

CHAPTER V. DISCUSSION

In this chapter, a discussion of the results is provided. Conclusions drawn by the researcher are also provided. The discussion and conclusions are provided in the order of the research questions presented. Study limitations and recommendations for further research are also provided.

For many items on the questionnaire the researcher believes the optimum answer would have been 100% agreement. For a few items the researcher believes the optimum answer would have been 100% disagreement. For other items on the questionnaire the researcher anticipated, and obtained, greater variability. The researcher uses terms like "substantial" and other word descriptors in describing values which are in accord with, or deviate from, these expectations. When the researcher uses the term "substantial" or other word descriptors for item results obtained he also usually includes a percentage or other comparable descriptor.

Discussion of Research Questions

Research Question One

Do experts in school psychology, and practicing school psychologists, agree or disagree with the definition of advocacy presented by the researcher, and what changes, if any, would they make to that definition?

Experts in school psychology and practicing school psychologists agreed with the definition of advocacy presented by the researcher, but they had some concerns about the terms ethical character and persuasion. The researcher's definition of advocacy is provided in parts in nine questionnaire items, all of which received majorities of agreement from survey participants, including practitioner participants. The researcher's definition of advocacy was provided in whole in two questionnaire items: a definition of advocacy for IDEA students, and a definition of advocacy for all students. Both items received majorities of agreement from survey participants, including practitioner participants.

The majorities of agreement from school psychologist practitioners for the researcher's definition presented in whole were substantial (above 80%). However, these majorities of agreement were below the majorities of agreement obtained from school psychologist practitioners for the component parts of the researcher's definition which stated that (a) school psychologists have an ethical obligation to be advocates for students, (b)school psychologists have an ethical obligation to speak up on behalf of students, (c) advocacy by school psychologists for students covered by the Individuals With Disabilities Education Act (IDEA) requires the capabilities necessary to develop individualized education programs (IEPs) that provide a free appropriate public education (FAPE) in the least restrictive environment (LRE), and (d) advocacy by school psychologists includes advocating for a FAPE for all students (all well above 90%). There was total agreement from school psychologists responding that school psychologists have an ethical obligation to be advocates for students. This was the only 100% agreement obtained to any item in the survey.

However, there were other components of the researcher's definition of advocacy to which survey participants were asked to respond that received percentages of agreement closer to the percentages of agreement received for the researcher's definition of advocacy presented in whole. These were the components of the definition that asserted that to be effective advocacy must be persuasive; that advocacy includes persuasion through logic; and that advocacy includes persuasion through the use of caring emotion. The assertion that advocacy includes persuasion through appropriate ethical character received percentages of agreement only slightly higher than these other components of the researcher's definition of advocacy. The word common to all of these assertions is persuasion. The researcher concludes that the percentages of agreement obtained for the researcher's definition of advocacy as proposed in whole were below the percentages of agreement obtained for these components of that definition because of, at least in part, the concern of participants over the meaning of persuasion and appropriate ethical character.

In addition to the commonality of the terms persuasion and appropriate ethical character as an explanation for the lower percentages of agreement obtained for these items than for other items representing components of the researcher's definition, there are the written comments provided by the participants in response to the researcher's definition of advocacy presented in whole, which express concern over the terms persuasion and ethical character. Although the number of these written comments by practitioners expressing concern was small, the researcher finds them to be significant when combined

with (a) the relatively lower percentages of agreement obtained for questionnaire

items containing these definitional terms; (b) the expressions of concern obtained

from some members of the focus group over how ethical character was to be

defined; and (c) the relatively lower percentages of agreement obtained for those

questionnaire items which assert that to be effective advocates school

psychologists must sometimes be adversarial with school staff and parents.

As one practitioner participant who disagreed with the researcher's

definition of advocacy put it, "Speaking up doesn't necessarily imply an

adversarial interaction or persuasion on the part of the school psychologist."

Judging by how survey participants responded to those questionnaire items that

addressed being adversarial as a component of advocacy, many were in agreement

with this participant. Only about 6 out of every 10 practitioner participants

responding agreed with the statement that to be effective advocates for students

school psychologists must sometimes be adversarial with school staff. Less than

half of practitioner participants responding agreed that to be effective as

advocates for students, school psychologists must sometimes be adversarial with

parents. The researcher concludes that, to the extent practitioners determined that

the word persuasion connoted being adversarial, they were less likely to be

accepting of the term persuasion as part of a definition of advocacy.

The problem that some focus group participants, and some survey

participants, had with the usage of ethical character was largely that it needed to be better defined, and the perceived related problem that if it was not better defined, it was a characterization subject to misuse. As one practitioner participant wrote, who was also critical of the usage of persuade in the researcher's proposed definition of advocacy and who gave the definition a neutral ranking, "I've known many very persuasive people whose ethical character was weak, at best." However, it is also true that no survey participant who strongly agreed with the researcher's proposed definition of advocacy presented in whole provided written comments critical of the usage of persuade or ethical character. Of practitioner participants responding to the researcher's proposed definition of advocacy presented in whole approximately a third strongly agreed.

The terms in the researcher's definition, including the terms persuade and ethical character, are meant to be linked. One cannot ethically persuade unless one persuades ethically.

By placing appropriate ethical character in his definition of advocacy as the most fundamental component of advocacy, the researcher meant: adherence by the school psychologist to the ethical principles of the profession, in this case the NASP *Principles for Professional Ethics*, with the qualification that the school psychologist's role as advocate needs to be clarified; and a commitment by the school psychologist to being *perceived* by others as behaving ethically. The most fundamental element of being persuasive, in addition to being rational and caring, is to be perceived as being ethical, whether or not one is adversarial. This being

94

ethical, and being perceived as being ethical, is most fundamental because it includes a commitment to advocacy, and a commitment to maintaining the capabilities for advocacy, as provided for in the NASP *Principles for Professional Ethics.* One cannot be a positive and effective school psychologist, which includes being rational and caring, unless as a school psychologist one maintains these ethical commitments. The researcher believes the way in which one focus group participant advocated for an abolition of her school's practice of corporal punishment is an excellent example of this ethic of advocacy.

Based on the quantitative and qualitative results of his research, the researcher offers the following revised proposed definition for the school psychologist as advocate, with new language in italics:

> School psychologists, as advocates, have an ethical obligation to "speak up" on behalf of students, including students with special needs who are entitled to a free appropriate public education (FAPE) (National Association of School Psychologists, NASP, 2000, p. 13). Speaking up, to be effective as advocacy, must be persuasive. *Ethical* advocacy is the process of attempting to *ethically* persuade others through logic, caring emotion, and ethical character. Of these three, the most fundamental is ethical character, because appropriate ethical character requires that school psychologists be committed *to following the NASP Ethical Principles, including,* as *those* Principles require, *being committed* to being advocates for students; and because appropriate ethical character also requires *a commitment by* school psychologists to being perceived as being ethical *persons* who advocate on behalf of students. *If school psychologists adopt and demonstrate appropriate ethical behavior, school psychologists will be persuasive.* Once school psychologists accept the obligation to be ethical advocates for students, school psychologists must also commit themselves to otherwise becoming *persuasive* speakers on behalf of students, if they are to be effective advocates for students. For students with disabilities covered by the IDEA, this includes developing and maintaining the capabilities necessary to participate in rational and caring conversations about how to create and maintain individualized education programs (IEPs) that provide these students with disabilities a free

95

appropriate public education (FAPE) in the least restrictive environment (LRE).

Research Question Two

How prepared do experts in school psychology, and practicing school psychologists, believe school psychologists are to fulfill their ethical obligation to be advocates for individual students with disabilities?

If being prepared means being sufficiently educated, then school psychologists do not believe that they are well prepared to fulfill their ethical obligation to be advocates. Less than half of the school psychologist practitioners responding agreed that they had received sufficient education in advocacy as part of their professional education in school psychology. Less than a quarter of the school psychologist practitioners responding agreed that they received sufficient ongoing professional education in advocacy. All of the focus group participants agreed that the profession could benefit from more ongoing education in advocacy, and as one focus group participant said about her prior professional education in school psychology,

> I don't recall, my training was awhile ago, but I don't recall advocacy being taught. I got taught how to give and interpret tests. I got taught how to run a staffing. Essentially, the basics. The nuts and bolts. I got taught consultation. Lots of consultation. And counseling. And program development. But not advocacy.

These expressions of belief by practicing school psychologists responding to the survey that they did not receive, and are not receiving, sufficient education in advocacy, are made even stronger by the strong majorities indicating in separate questionnaire items the importance of this education. Strong majorities (approaching 100%) of practicing school psychologists indicated that they were advocates for students and that professional education in school psychology should include ethics education and advocacy education. Strong majorities (over 95%) also believed that school psychologists employed by school districts could be effective and ethical advocates for students. However, substantially fewer (approximately 75%) of those school psychologists responding thought that school psychologists employed by the public schools could be as effective in their advocacy as school psychologists employed in other settings.

Despite the strong expressions of belief by school psychologist participants in the survey that ethics and advocacy education was needed and that they did not get enough of it, a substantial majority (approximately 80%) of these participants nonetheless also indicated that they had a good understanding of what it means to be a school psychologist advocate. The researcher concludes that majorities of practicing school psychologists in Colorado believe that they could have been better prepared to be advocates; that they could benefit from further preparation to fulfill their roles as advocates; but that a substantial majority of these practitioners also believe that they understand what it means to be prepared as, and to receive preparation in being, an advocate.

Research Question Three

As perceived by practicing school psychologists, and by school psychology experts, (a) what are the circumstances within which the ethical obligation for advocacy for individual students with disabilities manifests itself within the practice of school psychology, (b) what are the capabilities necessary for school psychologists to be effective advocates for individual students with disabilities, and (c) what are barriers to, and enablers of, effective advocacy by school psychologists on behalf of individual students with disabilities?

Part 1. The Advocacy Circumstances Items

What are the circumstances within which the ethical obligation for advocacy for individual students with disabilities manifests itself?

According to NASP, the circumstances within which the ethical obligation for advocacy for individual students, including students with disabilities, manifests itself is any circumstance in which the rights, welfare, and best interests, of students is primary. As stated in the NASP *Principles for Professional Ethics,*

> When the school psychologist is confronted with conflicts between client groups, the primary client is considered to be the child (p. 25).
> School psychologists consider children and other clients to be their primary responsibility, acting as advocates for their rights and welfare. If conflicts of interest between clients are present, the school psychologist supports conclusions that are in the best interest of the child (p. 25).

Focus group participants and school psychology practitioners responding to the survey generally agreed with the assertion that students are a school psychologist's primary clients. When asked directly whether a school psychologist's primary clients are students, 9 out of every 10 school psychology practitioners responding agreed, with 5 out of every 10 strongly agreeing.

98

However, when conflicts with other clients were introduced these levels of agreement were somewhat lower.

When the rights and welfare of students were presented absent potential conflict with other client groups, the students' rights and welfare were strongly supported. However when conflict, or potential conflict, with other clients, was expressly introduced this expression of support was somewhat reduced. When the conflict was with an implied school district client over the cost of services, support dropped substantially. When the prospect of costs for a needed private placement was raised, only 4 out of every 10 of the school psychologists responding agreed or strongly agreed with the assertion that a needed private placement should be recommended regardless of cost.

School psychologist practitioners responding to the survey did indicate, by strong majorities, that school psychologists should maintain their professional independence in making diagnostic determinations for students, including students with disabilities covered by the IDEA. And, 9 out of every 10 school psychologists responding agreed or strongly agreed that a school psychologist should advocate for students who were not receiving an appropriate education because of poor teaching practices, with almost 5 out of every 10 strongly agreeing. However, it was a smaller majority of school psychologists, slightly less than 8 out of every 10, who agreed or strongly agreed with the assertion that the primary role of a school psychologist is to be an advocate for students. And, it was a smaller majority still, only somewhat more than half, who agreed or strongly agreed with the assertion a school psychologist should advocate for students who are not receiving an appropriate education even if doing so is likely to cost the school psychologist his or her job. The number of school psychologist practitioners strongly agreeing with this assertion was about 1 out of every 10.

The researcher concludes that practicing school psychologists in Colorado, including school psychology experts, perceive the circumstances for advocacy for individual students, including students with disabilities, to be those circumstances where the rights, welfare, and best interests of the student are primary, in accordance with the NASP *Principles for Professional Ethics*. However, the researcher also concludes that school psychology practitioners in Colorado are not as certain about how to determine and how best to support the primary rights, welfare, and best interests of students, in circumstances where this determination and support is, or may be, in conflict with the rights, welfare, and best interests of others, including the school psychologist.

Part 2. The Advocacy Capabilities Items

What are the capabilities necessary for school psychologists to be effective advocates for students with disabilities?

In addition to being courageous, one focus group participant stated that school psychologist advocates needed to be good negotiators, collaborators, consultants, and team members. Another stated that they needed "the ability to see many perspectives and to help bring everyone together towards the common goal." Other focus group participants agreed.

Consistent with these focus group participants, school psychologists overwhelmingly agreed that effective advocacy requires school psychologists to collaborate with others, to be good listeners, and to work with teams to reach consensus. Substantial, although somewhat lesser majorities of school psychologists responding agreed that a school psychologist advocate should attempt to resolve conflicts between client groups in a manner mutually beneficial to all parties that protected the rights of all parties; and, that a school psychologist advocate needed to help others express differing views. These majorities of agreement were slightly above 90%.

The capability to be persuaded by others advocating on behalf of students, which might require collaboration, good listening skills, and attempts at consensus, was also recognized by a majority of school psychologist survey participants as a part of advocacy, although this majority of agreement (approximately 85%) was somewhat reduced. The majority of agreement drops somewhat further (to approximately 80%) when the assertion is made that to be effective advocates school psychologists must sometimes be capable of placing the needs of students above the needs of school systems. About 6 out of every 10 Colorado school psychologists responding agreed that a capability for advocacy is to be able to be adversarial with other school staff; and less than 5 out of every 10 Colorado school psychologists responding agreed that a capability for advocacy is to be able to adversarial with parents. Of school psychologists responding to these items, only about 13 out of every 100, and about 5 out of every 100, respectively, strongly agreed.

The researcher concludes that three of the capabilities perceived by school psychologists as necessary to be good advocates are the capability to collaborate with others, to be good listeners, and to be able to help teams reach consensus. However, the researcher also concludes that school psychologists in Colorado are somewhat less certain that they need to be capable of placing the needs of students above the needs of school systems in order to be effective advocates; and that they vary substantially in their views about whether they need to be capable of being adversarial with other school staff, and especially with parents, in order to be effective advocates for students.

Part 3. The Advocacy Barriers/Enablers Items

What are barriers to, and enablers of, effective advocacy by school psychologists on behalf of individual students with disabilities?

Uncertainty by school psychologists about the existence of conflict amongst and within a school psychologist's client groups and uncertainty by school psychologists about how to address this conflict, are primary barriers to effective advocacy by school psychologists on behalf of students, including students with disabilities. A primary enabler of effective advocacy would be the diminution of this conflict, a better recognition of it, and better skills in addressing it.

About one half of school psychologists responding agreed or strongly agreed that a school psychologist's advocacy for one student may sometimes conflict with the advocacy needs of one or more other students. Of school psychologists responding, only about 1 out of every 10 strongly agreed with this assertion, with a slightly greater number disagreeing or strongly disagreeing, and about one third being neutral. Thus, school psychologists responding as a group were uncertain about the extent to which their advocacy for one student could, or should, conflict with their advocacy for one or more other students. This despite the attorney expert's opinion that the most common ethical dilemma in special education is that resources allocated to one student, many times a student with special needs, often means that one or more other students will receive less resources.

Less than 3 out of every 10 school psychologists responding agreed or strongly agreed that if a school psychologist's advocacy for one student conflicts with advocacy for one or more other students, the school psychologist should advocate for the student with the greatest need. When the assertion is that the determinant of advocacy should be which student or students have the greatest legal rights, only 8 out of every 100 school psychologists responding agreed or strongly agreed. This despite the fact that students with disabilities have greater legal rights than those without disabilities, and that school psychologists and their school district employers are obligated to uphold these legal rights.

When school psychology practitioners were presented with the option of resolving conflicts between students by advocating for the outcome that would produce the greatest good for the greatest number of students, slightly less than 7 out of every 10 agreed or strongly agreed. That leaves approximately 3 out of every 10 school psychologists responding disagreeing, strongly disagreeing, or being neutral. Perhaps some of these who were in the minority are resolving conflicts between students on the basis of need or who has the greater legal rights, at least in some instances. In any case, the variation in how school psychologists responded to items addressing how conflicts between advocacy for students should be resolved indicates that a primary barrier to advocating for the rights, welfare, and best interests of the child who is a public education student, as required by the NASP *Principles for Professional Ethics,* including especially a student with a disability, is going to be when the rights, welfare, and best interests of one child conflict, or at least appear to conflict, with the rights, or best interests, or welfare of another child.

In addition to having students as clients whose rights, welfare, and best interests may be in conflict, school psychologists, according to the NASP *Principles for Professional Ethics* (2000), may have other clients:

> Throughout the *Principles for Professional Ethics,* it is assumed that, depending on the role and setting of the school psychologist, the client could include children, parents, teachers and other school personnel, other professionals, trainees, or supervisees (p. 15)....School psychologists typically serve multiple clients including children, parents, and systems (p. 25).

How are conflicts between these potential clients to be resolved? Again, according to the NASP *Principles for Professional Ethics* (2000),

> When the school psychologist is confronted with conflicts between client groups, the primary client is considered to be the child....If conflicts of interest between clients are present, the school psychologist supports conclusions that are in the best interest of the child (p. 25).

As previously discussed, it is within circumstances where conflicts between students and other client groups arise when the school psychologist's advocacy for students, consistent with the NASP *Principles* cited, becomes paramount. Also as previously discussed, it is the strong majority perception of practicing school psychologists in Colorado who responded to the survey that the rights, welfare, and best interests of students should be strongly supported, but that these majorities of support tend to be somewhat less strong in circumstances of potential conflict with other clients.

However, to what extent do practicing school psychologists in Colorado believe that they have other clients whose interests might conflict with the interests of their student clients? Of school psychologists responding, 7 out of every 10 agreed or strongly agreed that parents are a school psychologist's clients, and 7 out of every 10 agreed or strongly agreed that teachers are a school psychologist's clients. The agreement dropped slightly however when school psychologists were asked whether school systems are a school psychologist's clients. About one third of school psychologists responding disagreed, strongly disagreed, or were neutral when asked whether school systems were their clients.

The researcher concludes that while school psychologists in Colorado are more likely to see students as their clients than any other client group, parents and teachers are also viewed as clients by sufficient numbers of practicing school psychologists to foster substantial conflict, and hence to be a barrier to effective advocacy for students. The researcher also concludes that substantial conflict, and hence a barrier to effective advocacy for students, is also fostered when people who think that they should be clients, like parents, teachers, and school systems, are not viewed as clients by school psychologists. There are substantial minorities of school psychologists in Colorado who do not view parents, teachers, and especially school systems, as their clients.

Study Limitations

The researcher's study was limited to the state of Colorado. It was also limited to members of the primary state organization for Colorado school psychologists, the Colorado Society of School Psychologists (CSSP). A national study would, obviously, be more diverse. It may be that there would be differences in response based upon North, South, East, and West (farther west than Colorado) in the United States. The researcher does not know. The researcher's study was certainly limited in ethnic diversity. There were no African-American participants in the study, one Native-American participant, and only 5% Latino/a participants. The study participants were thus overwhelmingly Anglo, and, to a somewhat lesser extent, largely female (79%). A larger and more diverse sample would be helpful. However, the researcher did not see any

106

variations in his data that could be attributed to any diversity that was present in his study. Appendix M presents the demographic description of the research participants.

The response rate was 55%. Of those not responding, 10.5% did not respond because their questionnaires were returned as undeliverable. That leaves 34.5% that did not respond. It cannot be known for certain how those who did not respond would have responded. And, there is also no reason to believe that those not responding would have responded inconsistently with the 55% who did respond. To the extent there would have been differences in the opinions between these two groups, the researcher speculates that the non-responders would have been less committed to the advocacy role for school psychologists than were those who did respond.

To the extent that there was potential for bias amongst those 55% who did respond, the potential was in the direction of providing socially desirable responses. However, it was expected by the researcher that this bias would occur, given that the researcher was attempting to elicit favorable responses to the view that school psychologists are to be advocates to students. This bias is offset, however, by items in the survey questionnaire which attempt to gauge respondents' commitment to the obligation to be advocates for students, and which otherwise query their understanding of the advocacy role of school psychologists.

The researcher's survey questionnaire items could have been better or worse than the ones he constructed. The researcher went through an extensive process: from literature review, through focus group, through expert panel, through cognitive interviews, through pilot study, to construct his study-in-chief survey questionnaire items. But, more instances of all of these steps, using a more diverse sample, might have yielded richer survey questionnaire items. However, the researcher believes that even if this proved to be the case, the items obtained from such a diverse sample would address substantively similar issues as addressed by the researcher's survey questionnaire items.

Recommendations for Further Research

Do, or should, school psychologists have clients? If so, who is, or should be, the client, or clients? If a school psychologist has a client, or clients, should the school psychologist be an advocate for the client, or clients? If the school psychologist should be an advocate for a client, or clients, how should that advocacy be defined? However that advocacy is defined, should it be taught? If it should be taught, how should it be taught?

The NASP *Principles for Professional Ethics* (2000) state,

> The principles in this manual are based on the assumptions that 1) school psychologists will act as advocates for their students/clients, and 2) at the very least, school psychologists will do no harm. These assumptions necessitate that school psychologists "speak up" for the needs and rights of their students/clients even at times when it may be difficult to do so (p. 13).
> Throughout the *Principles for Professional Ethics*, it is assumed that, depending on the role and setting of the school psychologist, the client could include children, parents, teachers and other school personnel, other professionals, trainees, or supervisees (p. 15).

108

School psychologists attempt to resolve situations in which there are divided or conflicting interests in a manner that is mutually beneficial and protects the rights of all parties involved (p. 17).

School psychologists typically serve multiple clients including children, parents, and systems. When the school psychologist is confronted with conflicts between client groups, the primary client is considered to be the child. When the child is not the primary client, the individual or group of individuals who sought the assistance of the school psychologist is the primary client (p. 25).

School psychologists consider children and other clients to be their primary responsibility, acting as advocates for their rights and welfare. If conflicts of interest between clients are present, the school psychologist supports conclusions that are in the best interest of the child. When choosing a course of action, school psychologists take into account the rights of each individual involved and the duties of school personnel (pp. 25-26).

School psychologists' concerns for protecting the rights and welfare of children are communicated to the school administration and staff as the top priority in determining services (p. 26).

It seems problematic for a school psychologist, working in public education, to abide by these ethical principles. It is certainly possible for a professional, whether she/he be a school psychologist, or a physician, or an attorney, to have more than one client. However, a professional cannot ethically have clients whose interests conflict, at least not without full disclosure and informed consent. NASP attempts to resolve the conflict of interest problem by stating that, when client conflicts exist, "the primary client is considered to be the child" (p. 25). But, at the same time, the school psychologist is expected to "attempt to resolve situations in which there are divided or conflicting interests in a manner that is mutually beneficial and protects the rights of all parties involved"

(p. 17) and to "take into account the rights of each individual involved and the duties of school personnel" (p. 26).

However, by being employed by a public school district, the school psychologist has already entered into a professional relationship with the school district and with "children, parents, teachers and other school personnel [and potentially] other professionals, trainees, or supervisees (p. 15)," as identified by NASP (2000). The NASP *Principles for Professional Ethics* do not clearly describe how professional client relationships begin or end, but presumably all of the potential clients identified by NASP might presume themselves to be clients of the school psychologist once she/he began her employment with the school district.   That being the case, how could the school psychologist ethically and effectively continue with the student as a client, as NASP advises, once a conflict occurred between that student and her/his other clients, which might also include one or more other students? What about the trust, confidences, and expectations that have been established with these other clients? It seems problematic that other clients could be adequately honored and still honor the primary student client, for whom, as the primary client, according to NASP, the school psychologist is expected to primarily advocate. How does the school psychologist adhere to the NASP ethical admonition that she/he will "do no harm" in such circumstances? Even if the student is not the primary client, the potential for conflicts of interest exists.

The American Psychological Association (APA, 2002), which has a

Division 16 for school psychologists, has in its *Ethical Principles of Psychologists*

and Code of Conduct, at section 3.06, a requirement it places on its members for

addressing potential conflicts of interest:

> Psychologists refrain from taking on a professional role when personal,
> scientific, professional, legal, financial, or other interests or relationships
> could reasonably be expected to (1) impair their objectivity, competence,
> or effectiveness in performing their functions as psychologists or (2)
> expose the person or organization with whom the professional relationship
> exists to harm or exploitation.

And, at section 3.11, the APA (2002) addresses psychological services

delivered to or through organizations:

> (a)Psychologists delivering services to or through organizations provide
> information beforehand to clients and when appropriate those directly
> affected by the services about (1) the nature and objectives of the services,
> (2) the intended recipients, (3) which of the individuals are clients, (4) the
> relationship the psychologist will have with each person and the
> organization, (5) the probable use of services provided and information
> obtained, (6) who will have access to the information, and (7) limits of
> confidentiality. As soon as feasible, they provide information about the
> results and conclusions of such services to appropriate persons.

The only similar requirement to section 3.11 contained in the NASP

Principles for Professional Ethics, is found under the heading, "Relationships

with Employers," and states,

> Some school psychologists are employed in a variety of settings,
> organizational structures, and sectors and, as such, may create a conflict of
> interest. School psychologists operating in these different settings
> recognize the importance of ethical standards and the separation of roles
> and take full responsibility for protecting and completely informing the
> consumer of all potential concerns (p. 34).

It is unclear whether the NASP (2000) requirement for the school psychologist to take "full responsibility for protecting and completely informing the consumer of all potential concerns" (p. 34) would include all of the requirements of APA section 3.11, most particularly the requirements to disclose who is the school psychologist's client, or clients, and the relationship that the school psychologist will have with clients, other persons affected, and the organization. Absent such a discussion, it is hard to see how a school psychologist employed by a school district could meet her/his ethical obligation to avoid conflicts of interest with clients, either as those conflicts of interest would be defined by the APA or by NASP.

Despite his critical assessment of the ability of school psychologists to fulfill their historical and ethical role as advocates for students, the researcher strongly supports that role. However, it is unfair to school psychologists, and to the students and other clients for whom they may advocate, not to have sufficient clarity about how that role is to be fulfilled. The researcher has concluded that such sufficient clarity does not yet exist. If school psychologists are to have clients, then the NASP *Principles for Professional Ethics* need to more clearly prescribe how

- Client relationships are to be created and terminated;
- The terms of client relationships are to be defined;
- The terms of client relationships are to be communicated to clients;

- Conflicts of interest between multiple clients are to be determined, disclosed, and resolved, if school psychologists are to have multiple clients.

Sufficient clarity in the advocacy role for school psychologists cannot be obtained absent these ethical prescriptions.

The researcher does not pretend to know with certainty what these ethical prescriptions should be. He does know that NASP is now engaged in a 5 year process of addressing their policies and practices. Any changes to the NASP *Principles for Professional Ethics* should be as a result of an appropriate conversation amongst the membership of NASP. In the spirit of being a positive participant in that conversation, the researcher offers some suggestions for the consideration of the conversants about how client relationships might be better explained in the NASP *Principles*.

First, identify with greater specificity who or what may be a client of a school psychologist, and how that client relationship gets created. Thus, for example, if a school district is to be the client of a school psychologist it might be specified that the client relationship begins when the school psychologist signs a contract of employment with the school district. Similar sorts of specifics need to be included in the NASP *Principles* for all other potential clients of the school psychologist.

Second, if, as the NASP *Principles* prescribe, students or, in NASP's broader language children, are to be considered the primary clients of the school psychologist when conflicts between clients arise, then a better understanding of the ethical duty this is imposing on the school psychologist needs to be included in the NASP *Principles.* The NASP *Principles* prescribe that when such conflicts arise the school psychologist should seek an outcome that is in the best interests of the child. But this prescription does not seem to be sufficient guidance to help the school psychologist resolve circumstances where one child's best interests may be in conflict with a school district's best interests, or a parent's best interests, or a teacher's best interests, or any other actual or potential client of the school psychologist's best interests, or with the best interests of another child or group of children.

The NASP *Principles* promote resolution of such conflicts in a way that is mutually beneficial and protects the rights of all parties involved. This is an admirable goal that should be maintained; but in a finite world resources are finite and there are going to be some circumstances where the resolution of conflict is going to be that one or more will benefit more than one or more others. The NASP *Principles* cannot provide prescriptions so specific as to tell a school psychologist what she/he should do within the specific facts of specific conflicts. However, the NASP *Principles* could better prescribe whether the legal rights of a client should prevail when such conflicts arise, and whether a school psychologist's duty extends to losing her/his job in order to appropriately carry out her/his ethical duty to be an advocate for a client.

Third, the NASP *Principles* could prescribe that it is an ethical duty of school psychologists to seek out and obtain ongoing education in advocacy. The extent to which certain skills are necessary to being an ethical and effective advocate could also be more clearly stated and specifically organized in the NASP *Principles*. Given such provisions in the NASP *Principles;* and better provisions for determining who, or what, may be a client of a school psychologist; and better provisions explaining the parameters of a school psychologist's ethical duty to the primary student, or child client, training programs, both before and after a school psychologist begins her/his practice, would be in a better position to promote the advocacy role of school psychologists. The best model for doing so during the school psychologist's graduate school education would be, in the researcher's view, the clinical model. By *clinical model* the researcher means a model in which a school psychologist as a part of her/his graduate education in school psychology would receive, as a part of her/his education in providing school psychological services to clients in the community, case model education in advocacy and ethics as a part of that service education.

Finally, but nevertheless foremost, the researcher's quest began with a search for a definition of advocacy. With the help of many others, including members of the Colorado Society of School Psychologists, he found one. The NASP *Principles for Professional Ethics* needs to include a definition of advocacy. The researcher offers the definition of advocacy provided through this research to the conversants in the NASP revision process as one means for discussing how advocacy should be defined in the NASP *Principles for Professional Ethics.*

REFERENCES

Alper, S. K., Schloss, P. J., & Schloss, C. N. (Eds.). (1994). *Families of students with disabilities: Consultation and advocacy.* Boston, MA: Allyn & Bacon.

American Bar Association (2002). *Model Rules of Professional Conduct.* Chicago, IL: American Bar Association.

American Psychological Association (APA, 2002). *Ethical Principles and Code of Conduct.* Washington, DC: American Psychological Association.

Anderson, W., Chitwood, S., & Hayden, D. (1997). *Negotiating the special education maze.* Bethesda, MD: Woodbine House.

Board of Educ. v. Rowley, 458 U.S. 176 (1982).

Bonney, L. G., & Moore, S. (1992). Advocacy: Noun, verb, adjective or profanity. *Impact, 5*(2), 7.

Bush, G. W. (2004, December 3). President's remarks at the Signing of H.R. 1350. Retrieved on December 10, 2004, from http://www.whitehouse.gov/news/releases/2004/12/20041203-6.html

Cahill, B. F. (1986). Training volunteers as child advocates. *Child Welfare, 65*(6), 545-553.

Catterall, C. D., & Hinds, R. (1972). Child advocate – Emerging role for the
    school psychologist. *School Psychology Digest, 1,* 14-22.

Chapman, R. (2000). *The new handbook for special education rights.* Denver,
    CO: The Legal Center for People With Disabilities and Older People.

Chesler, M. A., Bryant, B. I., Jr., & Crowfoot, J. E. (1976). Consultation in
    schools: Inevitable conflict, partisanship, and advocacy. *Professional
    Psychology, 7,* 637-645.

Council for Exceptional Children (2003). *What every special educator must
    know: Ethics, standards, and guidelines for special educators.* Arlington,
    VA: Author.

Fiedler, C. R. (2000). *Making a difference: Advocacy competencies for special
    education professionals.* Needham Heights, MA: Allyn & Bacon.

Fish, S. (1980). *Is there a text in this class?* Cambridge, MA: Harvard University
    Press.

Garner, B. A. (Ed.). (2004). *Black's Law Dictionary.* St. Paul, MN: Thomson/
    West.

Herbert, M. D., & Mould, J. W. (1992). The advocacy role in public child
    welfare. *Child Welfare, 70*(2), 114-130.

Herr, S. S. (1991). Child advocacy in special education. In J. C. Westman (Ed.),
    Who speaks for the children? (pp. 147-173). Sarasota, FL: Professional
    Resource Exchange.

Hines, M. L. (1987). *Don't get mad: Get powerful! A manual for building advocacy skills.* Lansing, MI: Michigan Protection and Advocacy Service. (ERIC Document Reproduction Service No. ED 354 683).

Hyman, I., & Schreiber, K. (1974). The school psychologist as child advocate. *Children Today, 3,* 21-23.

Hyman, I., & Schreiber, K. (1977). Some personal reflections on the changing role of the school psychologist as child advocate. *School Psychology Digest, 6,* 6-10.

Individuals With Disabilities Education Act of 2004, 20 U.S.C. § 1400 *et seq.*

Jacob-Timm, S. (1999). Ethically challenging situations encountered by school psychologists. *Psychology in the Schools, 36*(3), 205-217.

Knitzer, J. E. (1976). Child advocacy: A perspective. *American Journal of Orthopsychiatry, 46,* 200-216.

Likert, R. (1932). A technique for the measurement of attitudes. *Archives of Psychology, 140,* 1-55.

McMahon, T. J. (1993). On the concept of child advocacy: A review of theory and methodology. *School Psychology Review, 22,* 744-755.

Mearig, J. S. (1974). On becoming a child advocate in school psychology. *Journal of School Psychology, 12,* 121-129.

Mills v. District of Columbia Board of Education, 348 F. Supp. 866 (D.D.C., 1972).

National Association of School Psychologists (NASP, 2000). *Principles for Professional Ethics.* Bethesda, MD: Author.

National Association of Social Workers (NASW, 2002). *NASW Standards for School Social Work Services.* Washington, DC.: Author.

Paul, J. L. (1977). The need for advocacy. In J. L. Paul, G. R. Neufeld, & J. W. Pelosi (Eds.), *Child advocacy within the system* (pp. 1-10). Syracuse, NY: Syracuse University Press.

Paul, J. L., Neufeld, G. R., & Pelosi, J. W. (Eds.). (1977). *Child advocacy within the system.* Syracuse, NY: Syracuse University Press.

Pennsylvania Association for Retarded Citizens v. Commonwealth of Pennsylvania, 343 F. Supp. 279 (E.D. Pa. 1972).

Rehabilitation Act of 1973, 29 U.S.C. § 504, 794.

Riley, P. V. (1971). Family advocacy: Case to cause and back to case. *Child Welfare, 50*(7), 374-383.

Stoecklin, V. L. (1994). Advocating for young children with disabilities. *Quarterly Resource, 8*(3). 1-35.

Svec, H. J. (1990). An advocacy model for the school psychologist. *School Psychology International, 11,* 63-70.

Westman, J. C. (1979). *Child advocacy.* New York: The Free Press.

Westman, J. C. (1991). *Who speaks for the children?* Sarasota, FL: Professional Resource Exchange.

Wright, P. W., & Wright, P. D. (2002). *From emotions to advocacy.* Hartfield,

VA: Harbor House Law Press.

APPENDICES

APPENDIX A

FOCUS GROUP CONSENT FORM

The purpose of this focus group is to research a proposed definition of advocacy for practicing school psychologists, most specifically advocacy for students with disabilities covered by the Individuals With Disabilities Education Act (IDEA). Your involvement will be to discuss and react to the researcher's proposed definition of advocacy. It is expected that this will take one to one-and-a-half-hours. This research is part of a dissertation study that will subsequently survey a random sample of practicing school-psychologist members of the National Association of School Psychologists (NASP) regarding their perceptions of their ethical role as advocates. There are minimal risks expected as a result of this study. In the unlikely event that you experience any anxiety or discomfort due to the discussion during the focus group, please notify the researcher.

The benefits of your participation in this focus group include the addition of your expertise to defining the advocacy role for school psychologists. School psychologists are required to be advocates by the NASP *Principles for Professional Ethics.* The results of the research will help practicing school psychologists, and NASP, to better understand the advocacy role of school psychologists. The focus-group discussion will last approximately one to one-and-a-half hours.

Information obtained through this focus group will be kept confidential by the researcher, though in a group discussion, confidentiality cannot be guaranteed. Your name will not be identified with any information collected during this study, without your written permission to do so. Questions or concerns about this study can be directed to: Dr. Kathy Green, University of Denver at 303.871.2490; Dr. Cynthia Hazel at 303.871.2961; or to Dr. Maria Riva, Chair, Institutional Review Board (IRB), at 303.871.2484. You may also contact the researcher, Charles M. Masner, at 303.674.7105 or at cmmasner@aol.com.

I understand that my participation in this focus group is voluntary and I can withdraw from the study at any time. I have read and understood the foregoing descriptions of the research project. I have asked for and received a satisfactory explanation of any language that I did not fully understand. I understand that there are two exceptions to the promise of confidentiality. If information is revealed concerning suicide, homicide, or child abuse and neglect, it is required by law that this be reported to the proper authorities. In addition, should any information contained in this study be the subject of a court order or lawful subpoena, the University of Denver might not be able to avoid compliance with the order or subpoena.

I agree to participate in this study, and I understand that I may withdraw my consent at any time. I have received a copy of this consent form.

_____   _____
Signature   Date

Please circle either Yes or No.

Yes, I agree to be audio taped.
No, I do not agree to be audio taped.

_____   _____
Signature   Date

This consent form was approved by the University of Denver's Institutional Review Board for the Protection of Human Subjects in Research on _____.

APPENDIX B

FOCUS GROUP PROTOCOL

<u>Introductions</u>	10 minutes

Explain focus group process:	5 minutes

Conversational

- Common experiences

- Honest perceptions

- Taping to assist in analysis of information

- Time limit, about 2 hours with a break

<u>Background</u>	5 minutes

Dissertation project, prelude to survey

Own interest in advocacy

Purpose: to research a proposed definition of advocacy for school psychologists. Most specifically for school psychologists working with students covered by the Individuals With Disabilities Education Act (IDEA).

Clarification questions.

Questions	40 minutes
Break	10 minutes
Questions	40 minutes

Closure/Thank you

APPENDIX C

FOCUS GROUP INTERVIEW GUIDE

Focus group participants will be told that the focus of the study is on advocacy for students with disabilities covered by the Individuals With Disabilities Education Act (IDEA). However, nothing prevents the participants from comparing and contrasting such advocacy for students without disabilities.

- Do you think being a child advocate is an appropriate ethical principle for school psychologists? Why or why not?

- Please share your views of the qualities necessary for school psychologists to be effective child advocates.

- Please share your views about how the practice of child advocacy by school psychologists could be improved.

- Please respond to the proposed definition of child advocacy for school psychologists.

APPENDIX D

EXPERT PANEL CONSENT FORM

The purpose of your expert review of potential questionnaire items is to aid the researcher in developing a survey questionnaire for the purpose of assessing the perceptions of school psychologists about their role as advocates, most specifically as advocates for students with disabilities covered by the Individuals With Disabilities Education Act (IDEA). You are being asked to review potential survey-item questions and comment on their worth. You are also being asked to offer any potential survey-item questions that you think would be appropriate. It is expected that this should take you no longer than 1 hour and it can be done at your convenience at a location of your choosing. This research is part of a dissertation study that will subsequently survey a random sample of practicing school-psychologist members of the National Association of School Psychologists (NASP), regarding their perceptions of their ethical role as advocates. There are minimal risks expected as a result of this study. In the unlikely event that you experience any anxiety or discomfort due to your expert review, please notify the researcher.

The benefits of your participation in the expert review of potential survey-questionnaire items include helping the researcher prepare a valid questionnaire for assessing the perceptions of practicing school psychologists about their role as advocates. School psychologists are required to be advocates by the NASP *Principles for Professional Ethics*. The results of this research will help practicing school psychologists, and NASP, to better understand the advocacy role of school psychologists. Your expert review can take as long as you wish, but the researcher does not expect that you will need to spend any more than one to one-and-a-half-hours to complete the review.

Information obtained from your review will be kept confidential by the researcher. Your name will not be identified with any information collected during this study, without your written permission to do so. Questions or concerns about this study can be directed to: Dr. Kathy Green, University of Denver at 303.871.2490; Dr. Cynthia Hazel at 303.871.2961; or Dr. Maria Riva, Chair, Institutional Review Board (IRB), at 303.871.2484. You may also contact the researcher, Charles M. Masner, at 303.674.7105 or at cmmasner@aol.com.

I understand that my participation in this expert review is voluntary and I can withdraw from the study at any time. I have read and understood the foregoing descriptions of the research project. I have asked for and received a satisfactory explanation of any language that I did not fully understand. I understand that there are two exceptions to the promise of confidentiality. If information is revealed concerning suicide, homicide, or child abuse and neglect, it is required by law that this be reported to the proper authorities. In addition, should any information contained in this study be the subject of a court order or lawful subpoena, the University of Denver might not be able to avoid compliance with the order or subpoena.

_____   _____

Signature   Date

I agree to participate in this study, and I understand that I may withdraw my consent at any time. I have received a copy of this consent form.

_____   _____

Signature   Date

Please circle either Yes or No.

Yes, I agree to be audio taped.
No, I do not agree to be audio taped.

_____   _____

Signature   Date

This consent form was approved by the University of Denver's Institutional Review Board for the Protection of Human Subjects in Research on _____.

APPENDIX E

EXPERT PANEL REVIEW LETTER

Dear _____

     Thank you for agreeing to review my draft, "The Ethic of Advocacy" (TEA) survey. As we have discussed, I am using the TEA to collect information for my dissertation. Please review the entire survey, observing the format, content of each section, wording of statements, and vocabulary use.

     You may make changes on the survey. Or, if you would like to rewrite statements or add statements that you believe would enhance the survey, please feel free to do so on the back of the page. If statements or information on the survey seem confusing to you, please indicate the confusing words, omitting or revising as you see fit.

     Based upon your experiences with advocacy for young people with disabilities in the public schools, covered by the Individuals With Disabilities Education Act (IDEA), please feel free to make revisions or make suggestions that you believe will enhance the understanding of the statements and encourage completion of the survey. If you have questions or ideas that you would like to discuss with me, please leave a message for me at 303.674.7105 and I will return your call.

     I have enclosed a stamped and self-addressed envelope for your convenience in returning the survey to me.

     Thank you.

     Respectfully yours,

128

APPENDIX F

COGNITIVE INTERVIEW CONSENT FORM

The purpose of this interview is to aid the researcher in developing a survey for the purpose of assessing the perceptions of school psychologists about their role as advocates, most specifically as advocates for students with disabilities covered by the Individuals With Disabilities Education Act (IDEA). You are being asked to review the proposed questionnaire and share your reactions to the questionnaire with the researcher. It is expected that this will require no more than 1 hour of your time. There are minimal risks expected as a result of this study. In the unlikely event that you experience any anxiety or discomfort due to the discussion during interview, please notify the researcher. The benefits of your participation in this interview to school psychology include the addition of your expertise in preparing a survey to assess the perceptions of practicing school psychologists about their role as advocates.

Information obtained through this interview will be kept confidential by the researcher. Your name will not be identified with any information collected during this study, without your written permission to do so. Questions or concerns about this study can be directed to: Dr. Kathy Green, University of Denver at 303.871.2490; Dr. Cynthia Hazel at 303.871.2961; or Dr. Maria Riva, Chair, Institutional Review Board (IRB), at 303.871.2484. You may also contact the researcher, Charles M. Masner, at 303.674.7105 or at cmmasner@aol.com.

I understand that my participation in this interview is voluntary and I can withdraw from the study at any time. I have read and understood the foregoing descriptions of the research project. I have asked for and received a satisfactory explanation of any language that I did not fully understand. I understand that there are two exceptions to the promise of confidentiality. If information is revealed concerning suicide, homicide, or child abuse and neglect, it is required by law that this be reported to the proper authorities. In addition, should any information contained in this study be the subject of a court order or lawful subpoena, the University of Denver might not be able to avoid compliance with the order or subpoena.

I agree to participate in this study, and I understand that I may withdraw my consent at any time. I have received a copy of this consent form.

This consent form was approved by the University of Denver's Institutional Review Board for the Protection of Human Subjects in Research on _____.

_____   _____

Signature   Date

Please circle either Yes or No.

Yes, I agree to be audio taped.
No, I do not agree to be audio taped.

_____   _____

Signature   Date

APPENDIX G

PILOT STUDY PROJECT INFORMATION LETTER

Dear Colorado School Psychologist:

Attached is a prospective national survey questionnaire to be used to gather information from a random sample of practicing school-psychologist members of the National Association of School Psychologists (NASP), about their ethical role as advocates; most specifically their role as advocates for students with disabilities covered by the Individuals With Disabilities Education Act (IDEA). You have been selected by the researcher to participate in a pilot study of this questionnaire. Information gained through this research will help practicing school psychologists, and NASP, to better understand the advocacy role of school psychologists. This survey is part of my dissertation research.

As a participant in this pilot study, your responses and recommendations will help me design the final questionnaire. Your suggestions for rewording or adding statements to improve the clarity of the questionnaire would be appreciated. Feel free to write in the margins or on the back of the survey. This brief survey will take you about 15 minutes to complete.

Your answers are confidential and will be aggregated with other responses. Responses will not be identified by name. When the study is completed and the data have been analyzed, any identifying information will be destroyed. By returning your completed questionnaire, you are giving consent for your responses to be utilized in the study.

Please complete and return the questionnaire in the stamped addressed envelope by March 11, 2006. If you have questions about this research, please feel free to contact: Dr. Kathy Green, University of Denver at 303.871.2490; Dr. Cynthia Hazel at 303.871.2961; or Dr. Maria Riva, Chair, Institutional Review Board, at 303.871.2484. You may also contact the researcher, Charles M. Masner, at 303.674.7105, or cmmasner@aol.com. Thank you.

Respectfully yours,

APPENDIX H

STUDY-IN-CHIEF PROJECT INFORMATION LETTER

(University of Denver Letterhead)

Dear CSSP Member:

      I invited you to participate in a questionnaire for members of the Colorado Society of School Psychologists (CSSP), about the role of school psychologists as advocates for students with disabilities; most specifically, students covered by the Individuals With Disabilities Education Act (IDEA). Your participation is voluntary. Information gained through this research will help school psychologists better understand the advocacy role of school psychologists. This survey is a part of my dissertation research.

      This questionnaire will take you about 15 minutes to complete. Your answers are confidential and will be aggregated with other responses. A number has been assigned to your questionnaire for coding in order to allow for confidential follow-up. No responses will be identified by name. When the study is completed, any identifying information will be destroyed. By returning your completed questionnaire, you are giving your consent for your responses to be utilized in this study.

      A $3.00 gift certificate is enclosed as a thank you for taking the time to consider participating in this study. If you have questions or concerns about this research, please feel free to contact: Dr. Kathy Green, University of Denver at 303.871.2490; Dr. Cynthia Hazel at 303.871.2961; or Dr. Maria Riva, Chair, Institutional Review Board (IRB), at 303.871.2484. You may also contact the researcher, Charles M. Masner, at 303.674.7105 or at cmmasner@aol.com.

      Please return your completed questionnaire in the enclosed self addressed and stamped envelope. Thank you.

      Respectfully yours,

This study, and this letter, have been approved by the University of Denver's Institutional Review Board for the Protection of Human Subjects in Research on April 14, 2006, and July 6, 2006.

APPENDIX I

STUDY-IN-CHIEF FOLLOW-UP LETTER

(University of Denver Letterhead)

Dear CSSP Member:

About two weeks ago you should have received a questionnaire, "The Ethic of Advocacy." I have not as yet received a completed questionnaire from you. This letter is a follow-up to my previous letter to you, renewing my invitation to you to participate in this study.

I know you must have many demands on your time, and I would therefore be very appreciative of the time you spent in completing and returning the questionnaire to me. If you wish to participate in this study, but you have misplaced or did not receive the questionnaire, please contact me, Charles M. Masner, at 303.674.7105 or cmmasner@aol.com and I will send you another questionnaire. Thank you again for taking the time to consider my request.

Respectfully yours,

This study, and this letter, have been approved by the University of Denver's Institutional Review Board for the Protection of Human Subjects in Research on April 14, 2006 and July 6, 2006.

APPENDIX J

INITIAL POTENTIAL SURVEY ITEMS

(Unless open-ended, or otherwise indicated, prospective survey items are Likert scale.)

Advocacy is the art and the science of persuasion.

An advocate is one who persuades others.

An advocate is a person of integrity.

An advocate should be a person of integrity.

An advocate interprets the world for others.

An advocate uses logic.

An advocate should be logical.

An advocate is compassionate.

An advocate should be compassionate.

School psychologists have an ethical obligation to be advocates.

School psychologists have an ethical obligation to be advocates for students.

When the rights of students conflict with the rights of others, the primary obligation of school psychologists is to the rights of students.

I am an advocate.

I am an advocate for students.

When the rights of students conflict with the rights of others, I place student rights first.

When the rights of a school district conflict with the rights of a student, I place student rights first.

When the rights of parents conflict with the rights of students, I place student rights first.

When the rights of students conflict with the rights of school staff, I place student rights first.

As a school psychologist, I have an ethical obligation to advocate for the rights of students.

As a school psychologist, I have an ethical obligation to advocate for a free appropriate public education (FAPE) for students with disabilities.

As a school psychologist, I have an ethical obligation to advocate for a free appropriate public education (FAPE) for all students.

As a school psychologist, my primary clients are students.

As a school psychologist, if conflicts exist between my student clients and any other clients I may have, my primary obligation is to my student clients.

Students with disabilities covered by the Individuals With Disabilities Education Act (IDEA), have a right to a free appropriate public education (FAPE).

Disagreements about what a FAPE should be for a student are not settled by the facts, but are the means by which those facts are settled.

When the school psychologist is confronted with conflicts between client groups, the primary client is considered to be the child.

If conflicts of interest between clients are present, the school psychologist supports conclusions that are in the best interest of the child.

School psychologists' concerns for protecting the rights and welfare of children should be communicated to the school administration and staff as the top priority in determining services.

Although all of a student's special needs may not be met within a public school system, there is a greater chance that they will be if a school psychologist advocate clarifies those needs.

A school psychologist should advocate for a student's right to learn.

Professional education in school psychology should include education in how to be an effective advocate.

Professional education in school psychology should include ethics education.

School psychologists need to learn as much as possible about how to advocate for children, so that children can reach their maximum potential.

The primary client of a school psychologist is the child, not the school system.

The primary role of a school psychologist is advocacy for children.

A school psychologist's primary role is child advocate.

The role of a school psychologist advocate is to help students get the educational services they need, even if school districts are reluctant to provide those services.

A school psychologist should advocate for educational change in order to meet the needs of all students.

In order to be effective child advocates, school psychologists must sometimes be adversarial with other school staff.

In order to be effective, child advocates, school psychologists must sometimes place the needs of students above the needs of the school system.

A school psychologist advocate should collaborate with others on behalf of students.

A school psychologist advocate should negotiate with others on behalf of students.

School psychologists should be educated about how to be successful child advocates.

A school psychologist child advocate should be adversarial with others on behalf of students.

A school psychologist child advocate must be professionally competent.

A school psychologist child advocate must engage in continuing professional development.

A school psychologist child advocate refrains from conflicts of interest.

A school psychologist child advocate recognizes conflicts of interest.

A school psychologist child advocate knows the NASP *Principles for Professional Ethics*.

A school psychologist child advocate knows how to apply the NASP *Principles for Professional Ethics*.

A school psychologist child advocate respects all persons.

A school psychologist child advocate respects human diversity.

A school psychologist child advocate informs student clients of school psychological services in advance of their administration.

A school psychologist child advocate attempts to resolve conflicts of interest in a manner that is mutually beneficial and protects the rights of all parties involved.

School psychologist child advocates respect the confidentiality rights of their student clients.

I received sufficient education in ethics as a part of my professional education in school psychology.

I received sufficient education in child advocacy as a part of my professional education in school psychology.

I receive sufficient ongoing professional education in ethics.

I receive sufficient ongoing professional education in child advocacy.

I have a good understanding of what it means to be an ethical school psychologist.

I have a good understanding of what it means to be a school psychologist child advocate.

A school psychologist child advocate should provide the diagnosis s/he thinks is accurate, even if a school administrator disagrees.

A school psychologist child advocate should recommend what is s/he thinks is best for a student, regardless of cost.

A school psychologist child advocate should find a student qualified for services if requested by a school administrator to do so.

A school psychologist child advocate should recommend needed counseling for a student, regardless of cost.

A school psychologist child advocate should recommend needed services for a student, regardless of whether the employing school district has those services available.

A school psychologist child advocate should recommend a needed private placement for a student, regardless of cost.

A school psychologist child advocate should attempt to develop appropriate programs for difficult students, even if administrators or other school staff don't want the student in school.

A school psychologist child advocate should speak up for children who are not receiving an appropriate education because of poor teaching practices.

A school psychologist should speak up for children who are not receiving an appropriate education, even if doing so is likely to cost the school psychologist his/her job.

School psychologists employed by school districts can be effective advocates for children.

School psychologists employed by school districts can be ethical advocates for children.

School psychologists employed by school districts should be advocates for children.

School psychologists employed by school districts can be as effective in their child advocacy as persons who are not employed by school districts.

School psychologists on the staff of school districts can be as effective in their child advocacy as school psychologists who are not on the staffs of school districts.

School psychologists employed by school districts can be more effective in their child advocacy than persons who are not employed by school districts.

School psychologists employed by school districts can be more effective in their child advocacy than school psychologists not employed by school districts.
I know what it means to be an effective advocate for children.

I know how to be an effective advocate for children.

Advocacy for children is an appropriate ethical principle for school psychologists.

School psychologists are better able to be advocates for children than other school staff.

Open-Ended Questions

Please provide your definition of child advocacy.

Please provide your view of the qualities necessary to be an effective child advocate.

Do you think being a child advocate is an appropriate ethical principle for school psychologists? Why or why not?

Please explain how your professional education in school psychology prepared you to be a child advocate.

Please explain in what ways your professional education in school psychology could have better prepared you to be a child advocate.

Please share your views about how the practice of child advocacy by school psychologists could be improved.

APPENDIX K

THE ETHIC OF ADVOCACY

PLEASE CIRCLE YOUR RESPONSE TO THE FOLLOWING ITEMS USING THE FOLLOWING SCALE:

1 = Strongly Disagree 2 = Disagree 3 = Neutral 4 = Agree 5 = Strongly Agree

		SD				SA
1.	School psychologists have an ethical obligation to be advocates for students.	1	2	3	4	5
2.	School psychologists have an ethical obligation to speak up on behalf of students.	1	2	3	4	5
3.	To be effective as advocacy, speaking up must be persuasive.	1	2	3	4	5
4.	Advocacy includes persuasion through the use of logic.	1	2	3	4	5
5.	Advocacy includes persuasion through the use of caring emotion.	1	2	3	4	5
6.	Advocacy includes persuasion by demonstrating appropriate ethical character.	1	2	3	4	5
7.	Advocacy by school psychologists for students with disabilities covered by the IDEA, requires school psychologists to develop and maintain the capabilities necessary to participate in rational and caring conversations about how to create and maintain individualized educational programs [IEPs] that provide these students a free appropriate public education [FAPE] in the least restrictive environment [LRE]. To what extent do you agree or disagree with this statement?	1	2	3	4	5

	SD				SA
8. I am an advocate for students.	1	2	3	4	5
9. I am an advocate for students with disabilities covered by the IDEA.	1	2	3	4	5
10. As a school psychologist, my primary clients are students.	1	2	3	4	5
11. As a school psychologist, if conflicts exist between my student clients and any other clients I may have, my primary obligation is to my student clients.	1	2	3	4	5
12. School psychologists' should communicate their concerns for protecting the rights and welfare of students to school administration and staff.	1	2	3	4	5
13. The rights and welfare of students should be the top priority in determining services for students.	1	2	3	4	5
14. Professional education in school psychology should include ethics education.	1	2	3	4	5
15. The primary client of a school psychologist is the student, not the school system.	1	2	3	4	5
16. The primary role of a school psychologist is to be an advocate for students.	1	2	3	4	5
17. School psychologists should advocate to help students get the educational services they need, even if school districts are reluctant to provide those services.	1	2	3	4	5
18. A school psychologist should advocate for educational change in order to meet the needs of all students.	1	2	3	4	5

	SD			**SA**

19. To be effective advocates for students, school psychologists must sometimes be adversarial with other school staff.

    1   2   3   4   5

20. To be effective advocates for students, school psychologists must sometimes place the needs of students above the needs of the school system.

    1   2   3   4   5

21. To be effective advocates, school psychologists should collaborate with others on behalf of students.

    1   2   3   4   5

22. A school psychologist's advocacy for one student may sometimes conflict with the advocacy needs of one or more other students.

    1   2   3   4   5

23. If a school psychologist's advocacy for one student conflicts with advocacy for one or more other students, the school psychologist should advocate for the student, or students, with the greatest need.

    1   2   3   4   5

24. If a school psychologist's advocacy for one student conflicts with advocacy for one or more other students, the school psychologist should advocate for the student, or students, with the strongest legal rights.

    1   2   3   4   5

    1   2   3   4   5

25. If a school psychologist's advocacy for one student conflicts with advocacy for one or more other students, the school psychologist should advocate for an outcome that will provide the greatest good for the greatest number of students.

26. To be effective student advocates, school psychologists must sometimes be adversarial with parents.

    1   2   3   4   5

	SD				**SA**
27. A school psychologist has an ethical obligation to advocate for a free appropriate public education (FAPE) for students with disabilities	1	2	3	4	5
28. A school psychologist has an ethical obligation to advocate for a free appropriate public education (FAPE) for all students.	1	2	3	4	5
29. Parents are a school psychologist's clients.	1	2	3	4	5
30. Teachers are a school psychologist's clients.	1	2	3	4	5
31. School systems are a school psychologist's clients.	1	2	3	4	5
32. If conflicts of interest between a school psychologist's clients are present, the school psychologist should support conclusions that are in the best interests of the student client.	1	2	3	4	5
33. When a school psychologist is confronted with conflicts between client groups, the primary client is considered to be the student.	1	2	3	4	5
34. School psychologists should be educated about how to be successful advocates.	1	2	3	4	5
35. A school psychologist advocate attempts to resolve conflicts of interest between client groups in a manner that is mutually beneficial and protects the rights of all parties.	1	2	3	4	5
36. A school psychologist advocate should provide the diagnosis s/he thinks is accurate, even if a school administrator disagrees.	1	2	3	4	5
37. A school psychologist advocate should recommend what s/he thinks is appropriate for a student, regardless of cost.	1	2	3	4	5

	SD				**SA**
38. A school psychologist advocate should find a student qualified for IDEA services if requested by a school administrator to do so.	1	2	3	4	5
39. A school psychologist advocate should find a student not qualified for IDEA services if requested by a school administrator to do so.	1	2	3	4	5
40. A school psychologist advocate should recommend what s/he believes are needed services for a student, regardless of whether the employing school district has those services available.	1	2	3	4	5
41. A school psychologist advocate should recommend what s/he believes is a needed private placement for a student, regardless of cost.	1	2	3	4	5
42. A school psychologist advocate should attempt to develop appropriate programs for difficult students, even if administrators or other school staff don't want the students in school.	1	2	3	4	5
43. A school psychologist should advocate for students who are not receiving an appropriate education because of poor teaching practices.	1	2	3	4	5
44. A school psychologist should advocate for students who are not receiving an appropriate education even if doing so is likely to cost the school psychologist his/her job.	1	2	3	4	5
45. School psychologists employed by school districts can be effective advocates for students.	1	2	3	4	5
46. School psychologists employed by school districts can be ethical advocates for students.	1	2	3	4	5

144

		SD				SA
47. School psychologists employed by school districts can be as effective in their advocacy as school psychologists who are employed in different settings.		1	2	3	4	5
48. A school psychologist advocate needs to be a good listener.		1	2	3	4	5
49. A school psychologist advocate needs to be 0able to help others express their views, even when the school psychologist disagrees with those views.		1	2	3	4	5
50. A school psychologist advocate needs to know how to work with teams in order to reach consensus.		1	2	3	4	5
51. A school psychologist advocate should be open to being persuaded by others who are advocating on behalf of students.		1	2	3	4	5
52. I received sufficient education in advocacy as a part of my professional education in school psychology.		1	2	3	4	5
53. I receive sufficient ongoing professional education in advocacy.		1	2	3	4	5
54. I have a good understanding of what it means to be a school psychologist advocate.		1	2	3	4	5

145

A Proposed Definition for the School Psychologist as Advocate: The IDEA Student Model

School psychologists, as advocates, have an ethical obligation to "speak up" on behalf of students, including students with special needs who are entitled to a free appropriate public education [FAPE] (NASP, 2000, p.13). Speaking up, to be effective as advocacy, must be persuasive. Advocacy is the process of attempting to persuade others through logic, caring emotion, and ethical character. Of these three, the most fundamental is ethical character, because appropriate ethical character requires that school psychologists be committed, as the NASP Ethical Principles require, to being advocates for students, and that school psychologists be perceived as being persons of appropriate ethical character who advocate on behalf of students. Once school psychologists accept the obligation to be ethical advocates for students, school psychologists must also commit themselves to otherwise becoming effective speakers on behalf of students, if they are to be effective advocates for students. For students with disabilities covered by the IDEA, this includes developing and maintaining the capabilities necessary to participate in rational and caring conversations about how to create and maintain individualized educational programs [IEPs] that provide these students with disabilities a free appropriate public education [FAPE] in the least restrictive environment [LRE].

55. The **Proposed Definition for the School Psychologist as Advocate** is appropriate for IDEA students.

SD				SA
1	2	3	4	5

Please explain your response.

56. The **Proposed Definition for the School Psychologist as Advocate** would be appropriate for all students, if all students, not just students with disabilities covered by the IDEA, were entitled to a free appropriate public education [FAPE] in the least restrictive environment [LRE], as determined by individualized educational programs [IEPs].

SD				SA
1	2	3	4	5

Please explain your response.

PLEASE CIRCLE THE APPROPRIATE RESPONSE

57. My gender is: male   female

58. My ethnicity is: African American/Black   Asian   Latino/a Anglo Other

59. My years of practice as a full time school psychologist are: 0-5   6-10   11 or more

60. My practice locale is: rural   urban   suburban   mixed (two or more specified locales of practice within the total years of practice) not applicable

61. My practice is: public private not applicable

62. My present professional role is best described as: student   practitioner supervisor teacher administrator retired other

PLEASE DESCRIBE ANY SUGGESTIONS YOU HAVE FOR FURTHER RESEARCH ON THIS TOPIC

THANK YOU VERY MUCH FOR YOUR HELP

APPENDIX L

ITEM CLUSTERS WITH RELIABILITY COEFFICIENTS

The Advocacy Definition Items, as presented in Table 1 on page 58, were:
- Item 1. Advocacy obligation
- Item 2. Speak up
- Item 3. Persuasive
- Item 4. Persuasive logic
- Item 5. Persuasive emotion
- Item 6. Persuasive ethical
- Item 7. FAPE/IDEA/LRE
- Item 27. FAPE/IDEA/LRE
- Item 28. FAPE/LRE – all students
- Item 55. Advocacy definition – IDEA students
- Item 56. Advocacy definition – all students

Cronbach's alpha = .80

The Advocacy Preparation Items, as presented in Table 2 on page 68, were:
- Item 8. Advocates for students
- Item 9. Advocates for students with disabilities
- Item 14. Ethics education
- Item 34. Advocacy education
- Item 45. School district school psychologists – effective advocacy
- Item 46. School district school psychologists – ethical advocacy
- Item 47. School district school psychologists vs. other
- Item 52. Sufficient education
- Item 53. Ongoing education
- Item 54. Advocacy understanding

Cronbach's alpha = .74

The Advocacy Circumstances Items, as presented in Table 3 on page 73, were:
- Item 10. Student as primary client
- Item 11. Student as primary obligation
- Item 12. Communicate concerns
- Item 13. Student as top priority
- Item 15. Student vs. system
- Item 16. Primary role as advocate

- Item 17. Advocate for services
- Item 18. Advocate for educational change
- Item 32. Student's best interests
- Item 33. Student as primary client
- Item 36. Diagnosis
- Item 37. Cost
- Item 38. Student as IDEA qualified
- Item 39. Student not qualified
- Item 40. Services available
- Item 41. Private placement
- Item 42. Appropriate programs
- Item 43. Poor teaching
- Item 44. Job jeopardy

Cronbach's alpha = .84

The Advocacy Capabilities Items, as presented in Table 4 on page 81, were:

- Item 19. Adversarial with staff
- Item 26. Adversarial with parents
- Item 20. Student needs
- Item 21. Collaborate with others
- Item 35. Resolve conflict
- Item 48. Listener
- Item 49. Other views
- Item 50. Consensus
- Item 51. Persuaded by others

Cronbach's alpha = .62

The Advocacy Barriers/Enablers Items, as presented in Table 5 on page 84, were:

- Item 22. Student advocacy conflict
- Item 23. Student with greatest need
- Item 24. Student with legal rights
- Item 25. Greatest good
- Item 29. Parent as client
- Item 30. Teacher as client
- Item 31. School system as client

Cronbach's alpha = .64

APPENDIX M

DEMOGRAPHIC DESCRIPTION OF THE SAMPLE

The Demographic Items

	Count	Percent
Gender		
Male	72	21.0
Female	271	79.0
Ethnicity		
Asian	6	1.8
Latino/a	17	5.0
Anglo	297	87.1
Other	21	6.2
Years as full-time school psychologist		
0-5 years	164	48.5
6-10 years	56	16.6
11+ years	118	34.9
Practice locale		
Rural	63	18.5
Urban	76	22.4
Suburban	108	31.8
Mixed	62	18.2
NA	31	9.1
Type of practice		
Public	279	81.8
Private	4	1.2
NA	45	13.2
Multiple	13	3.8
Professional role		
Student	51	14.9
Practitioner	224	65.5
Supervisor	4	1.2
Teacher	5	1.5
Administrator	10	2.9
Retired	18	5.3
Other	6	1.8
Multiple	24	7.0
Total	342	100.0

THE ETHIC OF ADVOCACY

_____

An Abstract of a Dissertation

Presented to

The College of Education

University of Denver

_____

In Partial Fulfillment

of the Requirements for the Degree

Doctor of Philosophy

_____

by

Charles M. Masner

June 2007

Co-Chairs:
Dr. Kathy Green
Dr. Cynthia Hazel

Abstract

School psychologists have an ethical obligation to be advocates for students. However, the ethical principles of the National Association of School Psychologists (NASP) do not define what it means for school psychologists to be advocates for students, except through the inferences that may be drawn from what school psychologists must be, and do, in order to comply with the NASP ethical principles. This dissertation proposed a definition of advocacy, which was then presented to a focus group of school psychology experts, to an expert panel, and then researched through a census survey of the Colorado Society of School Psychologists (CSSP), preceded by cognitive interviews and a small pilot study. This dissertation explored the perceptions of CSSP members regarding their ethical obligation to be advocates for students, including students entitled to a free appropriate public education (FAPE) under the Individuals With Disabilities Education Act (IDEA). Survey respondents were queried to determine their responses to the researcher's proposed definition of advocacy; how prepared they believed they were to be advocates for students, including students with disabilities; the circumstances within which the need for advocacy was presented; the capabilities necessary to be advocates; and the barriers and enablers of advocacy.

There were strong majorities of agreement with the researcher's proposed definition of advocacy, with the qualification that some concerns were expressed over the meanings of "persuasive" and "ethical character." There were strong majorities of agreement that school psychologists needed more education in advocacy in order to be better prepared as advocates. There were strong majorities of agreement that school psychologists should advocate for students; but survey participants also found advocating for students to be more problematic when the circumstances of this advocacy brought students into potential conflict with school district financial concerns and with job security for the school psychologist. Survey participants generally thought that good collaborative skills were necessary capabilities for effective advocacy by school psychologists, but they were divided over whether the capability to be adversarial with school staff and parents was necessary for effective advocacy. Responses from survey participants also indicated that conflicts between multiple clients of the school psychologist may be potential barriers to effective advocacy for students, and hence better resolution of such conflicts might enable better advocacy for students.